'MICK'

Jim Dudgeon was born in South Africa. He graduated in Modern History, and worked in a wide variety of jobs: as a musician, at a car-factory, as a motorway labourer, and as a barman. Having from early childhood had an interest in World War I aviation, and having to a large extent identified with Major Mannock, he travelled to France and Belgium to research the subject.

8

'MICK'

The Story of
Major Edward Mannock, VC, DSO, MC
Royal Flying Corps and Royal Air Force

James M. Dudgeon

[with forewords by]
Air Commodore Keith L. 'Grid' Caldwell
Lieutenant H. G. 'Clem' Clements
Group Captain Sir Douglas Bader

ROBERT HALE · LONDON

© *Copyright James M. Dudgeon 1981*
First published in Great Britain 1981
First paperback edition 1993

ISBN 0 7090 5169 7

Robert Hale Limited
Clerkenwell House
Clerkenwell Green
London EC1R 0HT

Printed and bound by
Interprint Ltd, Valletta, Malta

Contents

Illustrations

Between pages 64 and 65

CREDITS

Illustrations reproduced by permission of the following: The late Lt. Blaxland, 9; H.G. Clements, 12; J. Dudgeon, 1–3, 11, 13, 16–17; IWM, 15; Paul Leaman, 10; G.S. Leslie, 14; Mannock family, 4, 7, 8, 19; Dave Roberts, RAF Museum, 18; Les Rogers, 5; D. Whetton, 6.

Acknowledgements

My sincere thanks to the following people who have given up so much of their time to assist in the writing of this book. Without their energy and enthusiasm, the task would have proved impossible.

Air Commodore Keith L. 'Grid' Caldwell, RNZAF.
Lt H. G. 'Clem' Clements.
Lt W. B. 'Twist' Giles.
The late Lt Lionel B. Blaxland.
The family of Edward Mannock, with special thanks to Michael Mannock.
Mrs Eveline Inglis, widow of the late Lt Donald C. Inglis.
Miss Jean Inglis.
John Garwood. Aviation Historical Society of New Zealand.
The Imperial War Museum. G. Clout and E. Hine.
The Royal Air Force Museum. Dave Roberts.
The Public Records Office.
Fellow members of Cross and Cockade (GB); The Society of World War One Aero Historians. Paul Leaman, Les Rogers, Stuart Leslie, Bill Vandersteen, Dennis Hylands.
Militargeschichtliches Forschungsamt.
Deutsche Luftfahrt—Archiv.
The late Douglas Whetton.
Miss Valerie Murfin.
Chaz Bowyer.

Angus and Nancy Stewart.
Miss Pat McCarthy of MAP Ltd.
Roy Yates of *Radio Modeller* magazine.
Royal Aircraft Establishment, Farnborough.
Roy Aspin of the Institute of Geological Science, London.
S. de B van C for the use of his collection of letters, diaries
and photographs.
Sally, Neil and Jules Munro.
Giltspur Engineering (Graphics).
T. R. Dudgeon.
'Muffin'.

My special thanks to the Vergez family of Beuvry, Pas de
Calais, France. If not for their kindness and hospitality,
my rain-soaked days searching the fields of France would
have amounted to nothing.

And to the publishers for permission to quote from *Five
Years in the Royal Flying Corps* (Flying Fury), by James
McCudden VC (published by John Hamilton), *The
Personal Diary of 'Mick' Mannock VC*, annotated by
Frederick Oughton (Neville Spearman) and *Fighter Pilot*
by 'McScotch' (Routledge & Kegan Paul Ltd).

Edinburgh   J. M. DUDGEON

Foreword
by Air Commodore Keith L. 'Grid' Caldwell
MC RNZAF.

Although some sixty-two years have passed since the end
of the Great War of 1914–18, the last decade has shown an
upsurge of interest in that period and especially in the
fliers of that war. They are legendary figures now, and
their deeds are still capable of stimulating interest in the
younger generation of today. Knowing the interest that
exists about the leading figures of those far-off days, I am
pleased to write these introductory remarks to this biography of 'Mick' Mannock, a man I knew so well and, with
many others, regarded so highly.

I first met Mannock in mid 1917 while visiting 40
Squadron at Bruay in northern France. We had a long
conversation, and I was immediately impressed by his
dedicated keenness and fervent desire to shoot down as
many German aircraft as possible. He already had quite a
score to his credit and had been awarded the Military
Cross.

In early 1918, I met him again at London Colney, where
a new training squadron, No 74, was being formed. I was
fortunate enough to be the new CO and was delighted that
Mannock was the senior flight commander in charge of 'A'
Flight. With Mannock to give a lead to the men, I felt that
we might have quite a good 'spin' when we went to France
and got up against the enemy. And so it was to be.

Mick was a very human, sensitive sort of chap; he did
not hate people or things at all. He has, however, gained
the reputation of being a fervent 'Hun-hater'. I believe

that this hatred was calculated or assumed to boost his own morale and that of the squadron in general. This was the sort of war-going outlook it rather paid to have. Why was he so successful? An extraordinarily good shot and a very good strategist, he would place his flight high against the sun and lead them into a favourable position where they would have the maximum advantage. Then he would go down quickly on the enemy, slowing down at the last possible moment to ensure that each of his followers got into a good firing-position. He was keenly interested in the success of his flight, not only his own record of kills. Three months of dedicated work brought him a well deserved promotion. When he was posted to the command of 85 Squadron, his influence was soon established, and standards in that unit went up under his leadership and the example he gave. What has been said of Mannock—that he spared time and had the patience to build confidence in his inexperienced pilots—is very true. It's sad to think that he was doing just this when he met his most tragic death.

Some critics have written that Mannock's score of seventy-three enemy aircraft should in fact be less, but it should be remembered that he passed on some of his own kills to his men as an extra encouragement—I would estimate at least four or five. But what does this all matter now? What does matter is that he was a wonderful chap and that he had a great personal record. How fitting it was that he received a posthumous VC after the war was over.

In closing, I wish to say that I have enjoyed writing these comments about not only a leading pilot of World War I but a MAN, much older than he should have been for the stresses he bore, a warm, lovable individual of many moods and characteristics. I shall always salute his memory.

Auckland   KEITH L. CALDWELL
New Zealand

Foreword
by Lt H. G. 'Clem' Clements, Alberta
Regiment attached RFC and RAF.

Amid the horrors and tumult of war, there will always be a number of people whose gallantry and dedication to their particular task in the conflict inspires writers to tell their stories long after their deeds have passed into history. Major Edward 'Mick' Mannock was among those in World War I who will never be forgotten, and I have always considered that I was privileged to have known him and flown with him in 74 Squadron.

The fact that I am here sixty-two years later to write this foreword, is due to his high standard of leadership and the strict discipline on which he insisted. We were all expected to follow and cover him as far as possible during an engagement and then to rejoin the formation as soon as that engagement was over. None of Mick's pilots would have dreamed of chasing off alone after the retreating enemy or any other such foolhardy act. He moulded us into a team, and because of his skilled leadership we became a highly efficient team. Flight members who left the formation on patrol were always duty-bound to show a real reason for leaving their post—i.e. engine or gun faults, and Mick always satisfied himself that such information was correct.

Our squadron commander, Keith Caldwell, in a recent letter to me, said that Mannock was the most skilful patrol leader in World War I, which would account for the relatively few casualties in his flight compared with the high number of enemy aircraft destroyed. Incidentally, I have to thank the author for putting me in touch with Caldwell after sixty-two years.

I must compliment the author on his dedicated research into the life and flying-career of 'Mick' Mannock. I know of the long hours spent and the trouble taken to verify his facts.

Apart from occasional visits to see Mick when he was commanding 85 Squadron, I knew little of him after he left 74. The last time I saw him was on 25th July 1918, the day before he was killed. Taffy Jones and I went over to 85 to have tea with him, and most of the time he appeared to be his normal cheerful self. That is how I will always remember him: a MAN among men.

Leicester,
England.

H. G. CLEMENTS

Foreword

by Group Captain Sir Douglas Bader,
CBE, DSO, DFC, RAF

To youngsters like myself, when I joined the Royal Air Force in 1928, the names of Mannock, Ball, McCudden, Bishop, von Richthofen and others were an inspiration. I read all about these great fighter pilots of World War I. Their methods and tactics stayed in my mind when I started to fight in the air myself in May 1940.

Their three golden rules for a fighter pilot were:

1. Get above your opponent and the advantage is yours.
2. Get up-sun of your opponent and he won't see you.
3. Get close before shooting and you won't miss.

These principles remained true whether one was flying a Fokker or an SE 5A in 1917, a Spitfire or an ME 109 in 1940.

This is the first biography I have read about Mannock. I found it fascinating. The author clearly has taken great trouble with his research. He tells us the background and upbringing of his subject before he became famous. It is in this respect that I like this book. There is a tendency to regard famous people as folk apart and to think of them only in their heyday. To discover that they started life as ordinary people makes them real.

I commend this book as a valuable addition to the bookshelf of any military aviation enthusiast.

London   DOUGLAS BADER

For Rose

Prologue: France, 26th July 1918

Dawn broke on this day as it had on all the other wasted days of war. Men stood down from the duties of the night and left the monotony of the day to their equally exhausted comrades.

For the men in the trenches between Mont Bernanchon and Pacaut Wood, however, this day would prove to be somewhat different. As they passed tea and dry rations from man to man, they could have little idea of the tragedy about to take place before their eyes. Cupping hands around cold tea-mugs, few even bothered to look upwards at the sound of an approaching aircraft.

Leutnant Ludwig Schopf settled down in his roomy cockpit to avoid the tearing propeller slipstream and surveyed the churned landscape passing below. For Schopf, the war on this sector had also become boring and uncomfortable. Rarely did he see enemy fighters or anti-aircraft fire—that was reserved for his brother pilots on the more lethal fronts. Day after day he would fly over the same course at the same time, looking through sleep-weary eyes for signs that the British might be preparing to take this particular part of the war seriously. In the distance he could see the lines and the spot where he would make his diving turn—the spot where he always made the same diving turn. A few low passes over the Tommies, Hein, his observer, would fire off a few long bursts, and that would be it for yet another day. As usual the Tommies would react in the same manner. Most would run or fall into the safety of the shell-hole; some would fall wounded or dead; some would make the effort of firing back at this intruder into their moment of peace. Schopf threw a glance at the bundled figure of Hein in the rear cockpit and then eased his heavy machine over in a gentle turn down towards the waiting British. Two rapidly approaching specks in the distance passed the edge of his vision unseen.

Bracing himself against the edge of the cockpit rim, Sergeant Joseph Hein checked his gun and the large drum of ammunition clamped to its side. Soon the stomach-churning descent would be over, and he could start his short and almost ineffective offence against the half-sleeping infantry. At a height of 100 feet, both he and Schopf would be difficult targets for the few Tommies who would actually fire back. The British had never affected his nerve as he moved his gun back and forth over the fleeting figures.

As Schopf turned his machine around for a second pass along the line, Hein was startled by a thunderous hammering. In horror he turned to see the nose of a dark brown fighter which had sharked its way up from below; he watched the muzzles of its guns explode with streams of fire, and then he sank lifeless into his seat as the fighter blurred overhead. Schopf turned an instant later to see a second machine only feet from his tail, its fire churning up the fuselage and covering him in petrol. Frantically, the German kicked at the shattered controls but then resigned his life to the scorching flames as they filled his lungs. He fell over the control-stick and sent the burning mass down to crash near a village called Lestremme.

As the German machine burned on the ground, the pilot of the second fighter caught his breath and tried desperately to control his overflowing emotions. A mixture of fear, delight and horror filled his being as he watched the burning enemy—fear at the thought of how close he had come to ramming the German, delight at his first success in the air, horror at the sight of the pilot's face as his machine was cut to bits around him. Putting these thoughts behind him, the young pilot ignored the heavy ground-fire and flew towards his leader.

Seeing his leader's beaming smile and wave, Lieutenant Donald Inglis sensed a new, stronger emotion welling up inside him. He looked at the ruddy, muffled face only yards away and, for the first time in his life, realized what one man could feel for another. In the short space of three weeks, that one man had infected them all in the Squadron with a similar feeling. He had taught them, led them, saved them from death and captured their lasting friendship. The Squadron had gone from strength to strength under his command; new bonds had been tied, new trusts had been formed, and all this from a unit which had all but given up under its previous Commanding Officer. So great an effect had he had on them that even the meekest would now fly into any number of Germans, so long as he was there. That man alongside gave Inglis the nerve he needed—with him you were safe, no matter what the odds.

Crossing the lines, the fighters were met with a massive volley of ground-fire, and tracers flashed around them with a wicked glint. Distracted for a moment, the young pilot lost sight of his leader but soon caught sight of him diving and weaving towards the remains of a small wood. On reaching the wood, the leading fighter turned side-on to Inglis and displayed a sight which horrified him beyond description: flames. At first it was only a small blue-white flicker, a gleam which suddenly burst forth into a torrent flowing over the body of the machine. Staring in disbelief, Inglis watched as the doomed aircraft went down in a series of turns to crash near the funeral pyre of his own victim.

Flying straight and level, hypnotized by this seemingly impossible sight, Inglis remembered little else until he too slammed into the trenches. Covered in petrol from his shattered tank, he was dragged shouting from the wreck, hardly able to walk. Soldiers of the Welsh Regiment bundled him into a dug-out and tore off his fuel-sodden clothes. Through mouthfuls of choking rum, the trembling young man coughed out his last words of that day.

"They killed him. The bastards killed my major. They killed Mick."

Before collapsing into a shock-induced sleep, Inglis raised himself in one last effort to look out on the burning remains of 'his Major'. The oily black pall marked the dying-place of Major Edward 'Mick' Mannock, fighter, leader, tactician and ruthless killer. But none of these descriptions went through the mind of Donald Inglis. He could think only of the kind and gentle man who helped everyone, the sensitive musician, the devout Socialist, who loved his fellow man and longed for a more just and gentle world. These conflicting facets of Mannock's character were a mystery to Inglis. He would have to wait twenty years for part of his friend's story to be told; he would die of old age before the answers to this enigma of the Great War would be found.

1
The Corporal's Son

On 24th May 1887 Julia Mannock gave birth to her third
child, a son named Edward. For some reason this child
gave her a special feeling, one which she had not experienced at the births of her other children. Both Jessie
and Patrick were good children whom she loved dearly,
but what, she thought, was special about young Eddie?
The answer sprang to life at the entrance of her husband.
Corporal Edward Mannock was drunk, drunk on the
beer she had bought to celebrate the new birth. He had
started on the bottles hours before and had shown no
interest in her birthpains. To him the child was yet
another burden on his overladen back, yet one more responsibility. Julia looked away from the dishevelled,
drink-laden man and returned her gaze to the baby's light
blue eyes. Those eyes were also special, she thought, cold
and piercing but warm and inviting at the same time. This
child would have the love she now found herself incapable
of giving her husband. He would become her life. The few
years in which he would depend on her attentions would be
short reward for her years of devotion; after that she might
have nothing left in life, but those years would be something. Looking into the depth of his young eyes, she
thought back to those far-off times of happiness.
  She had been a fine-looking girl, everyone said so. The
soldiers who flocked to the village of Ballincollig from
Cork had pursued her with zeal, but only one had any
effect on her, the Corporal. It had been the summer of
1881, one of the hottest in memory. He stood at the corner
of the single main street boasting to his men of some great

feat in the past. She had not seen the boastful side however, only the fine, tall figure of a Royal Scots Grey in full dress uniform, the very picture of a soldier, the very type she had seen so often in books. As she approached the chattering soldiers, Mannock had come forward and looked down at her small form with his fixing gaze. That had been the moment when she knew for certain that this man would become her husband.

The courtship had been short and dynamic, full of fiery emotion and tender loving. For the first time in her life she was truly happy; for the first time in his life, he was opening up to another person and admitting the faults which he had in plenty. At this time he was known as Corringhame, having enlisted under his mother's maiden name. Nervously he explained that some event in his past, too terrible to speak of, had driven him away from the family he loved in England. What that dreadful event was, Julia would never know. Her love for the Corporal was too great for her to bother with such matters. He was a good man, from a fine family—that was all she felt concerned with. His father was the editor of a Fleet Street paper, his uncle a friend of the Royal Family;[1] she put his secret aside and looked to their future together. Whatever the man might have been was irrelevant. She had seen the changes in him: no more nights with his rough army men, no more drinking himself into lunatic states. Mannock proposed, and she fell even more deeply in love.

They married in the spring of 1882 and left almost immediately for Mannock's new posting in Glasgow. Julia settled easily into her new life in the army married quarters. Here she experienced a way of life superior to her poverty-ridden existence in Ireland.

She decorated their home with great zeal: curtains, tablecloths, wallpaper; nothing was too good for her corporal. Every night he would return to a well cooked meal and the almost worshipful attentions of his wife.

[1] George Mannock had taught the Prince of Wales to play billiards.

Their nights were spent quietly at home, before a blazing fire, arm in arm. The big rough man she had known was changing—he became happy in his work and came to love the peace of a family life. Leaving their home when the Regiment was posted to Edinburgh brought some sadness, but to Julia Mannock this was little to give in return for her man's love.

Edinburgh was initially to give them the same happiness, but events far away were combining to change all that.

Egypt, one of Britain's most important outposts since the building of the Suez Canal, was being threatened by revolt. The Egyptian people had become resentful at the interference of the French and British and rose against the Empires in 1881 under Arabi Pasha. Ships of the British and French fleets were sent to ensure the defeat of the revolt, but when the Egyptians started murdering Europeans and building fortifications, the French withdrew. The Royal Navy bombarded the fortifications, and in 1882 a force under Sir Garnet Wolseley defeated the Pasha's forces at Tel el Kebir. It was at this battle that Corporal Mannock regained his taste for adventure. For ten months he rode into action on camel-back, charging the enemy with sabre in hand.

He returned to his wife and newly born daughter, Jessie, in December 1882. The comforts of home were most welcome after months of campaigning, but in the end they only served to nurture the seed of dissatisfaction in Mannock's soul. His uniform, decorated with the Egyptian Star and Medal, was worn for all to see, and although Julia failed to see it at the time, that uniform was once again becoming the most important thing in Mannock's life.

Four years later the family arrived in Aldershot, where in March 1886 Patrick Mannock was born. Although not unpleasant for Julia, the marriage was losing some of its initial spark. The Corporal was still a responsible husband, but his drinking had started again to a small extent.

In 1887 the Mannocks were moved to Ireland for the annual military manoeuvres, and it was during this stay that Edward was born, in Cork, on 24th May.[2] Left without her husband for seven months, Julia spent her time visiting relatives to show off the children of whom she was so proud.

At the end of the Curragh manoeuvres, Corporal Mannock rejoined his family at Newbridge Camp near Dublin and heard that his service in the army was completed and that he was free to leave. Happy that her husband might now follow a more safe and secure profession, Julia failed to notice the Corporal's air of despondency as he took off his uniform for the last time.

Time expired, Corporal Mannock left the army and moved to Highgate, London, with his family. Forty pounds saved during his service was all they had to live on until Mannock settled into a new position. Eighteen months passed, and still the ex-soldier had no permanent employment. Drifting from job to job, he became more dissatisfied with civilian life. His home life became unbearable: three children to care for, debts, lack of sufficient food—everything seemed to be against him.

In an effort to get away from it all, Mannock left home to spend a weekend with relatives in Liverpool. While there, he met with a recruiting unit and decided there and then to re-enlist; this time however, it was under his own name. His honesty in the matter and his soldierly qualities overcame the problems posed by his former fraudulent enlistment, and he became a soldier once more: Trooper Edward Mannock of the Fifth Dragoon Guards. Julia was secretly furious at the news which her beaming husband brought back with him; he was off to India to join his new regiment, and Julia and the children would follow on.

In Meerut, in May 1893, the newly promoted Corporal

[2] Although many writers have quoted Brighton, England, as Mannock's place of birth, all the family documents refer to Cork. The first weeks of his life were spent near Cork in a tumble-down house which was situated over a cowshed.

Mannock welcomed his family into India. Seven months of separation had rekindled some of the magic between the couple. Julia saw him once again as the dashing cavalryman, now heavily tanned by the Indian sun, resplendent in his fine uniform. For the first time in years, life turned down a pleasant path for the Mannock family. Even young Edward, they noticed, was coming out of his shell to an extent.

Years of his mother's attentions and the lack of fatherly discipline had taken its toll. 'Eddie' had spent the first six years of his life acting as the focal-point for his mother's frustrated love, pandered-to and over-protected. India gave him a well earned rest from his mother. While she basked in the Corporal's new interest in her, Edward set about exploring what was to him an unknown quantity—freedom. Unlike most children of his age, he did not take advantage of the lack of parental supervision but spent his time quietly by himself exploring the mysteries of his new home. A fascinating place for any stranger, India took on a special significance for the young boy. Filled with all manner of strange sights, the large sprawling country drew his interest as a sponge draws water. For the first time he was observing and thinking independently, and he found a satisfaction in his new-found ability to reason and learn for himself. Question after question filled his fertile brain. What, who, how, where, why—these words punctuated his every conversation.

Ignoring the sometimes cruel comments of the other children, Edward would slip off alone to one of his private places where he could not be interrupted. There he would read, observe his surroundings and think out what he had taken in. Life was good for young Eddie Mannock at this time. He felt the world under his feet and thought it a great miracle to be explored daily.

His world and its wonders also opened up his mind to the less pleasant aspects of life. Why, he asked, did the soldiers' children run barefoot and ragged while those of the officers dressed well? Officers and civil servants lived in fine bungalows, while his family lived with four others in a small wooden hut. Men were divided into sections: officers, ranks and servants—surely this could not be right? Edward saw men starved and beaten, mocked because of their various afflictions, treated as if not belonging to the same species. The priest taught that all men were created equal; why then were there separate churches for different classes of men? No one would answer his questions about the injustice so prevalent around him, and the books which he devoured daily went only part of the way towards explaining this confusion of ideas. Unable to relate to the life-style in which he found himself, Edward withdrew into his fertile mind and became an even greater reader and thinker. Safe inside his womb of thought, the questioning young boy set about learning those things which would help him to destroy this evil and unjust world. He was incapable of explaining it all to himself; he knew it was wrong, and that was that. Plans formed in his dreams: he would become educated and leave this all behind him; then, once he had the means to achieve his aims, it must all change. Packing books into his satchel, Edward clenched his jaw in a determined re-affirmation of his plans and strode purposely towards the barracks he so hated. It was 1897, and the bottom was about to fall out of his world; within two days he would be completely blind.

That night after supper the Mannocks settled into their individual corners, amusing themselves in various ways. Corporal Mannock sat in his high-backed chair, pipe clamped firmly between strong jaws. His thoughts of going out for a few beers were disturbed by the continual movements of his son Eddie. His constant movements around the table and from lamp to lamp were too much for the quick-tempered father.

"What the hell is it yer up to now, boy, tell me?"

"It's the lamp Dad. I can't see what I'm doing properly."

"Nowt wrong wi' the lamp. It's them daft books you read, tiring the eyes. It'll be flowers and birds or the sun and stars again, I wager. Fine rubbish for a boy of your age.

You'll be through playing' wi' the girls next door."

Knowing full well that no explanation would convince the angry man, Eddie packed his books and headed for bed, yet another of his refuges from the world.

In the early hours of the next morning he was once again faced with the task of convincing his father. A burning pain in both eyes had forced him from sleep, his tears of pain doing little to help his case against the now furious Corporal. Within twenty-four hours the Corporal would need little convincing. Not even he could argue with the opinion of the regimental surgeon.

"It will have come from the dust I suspect—what we call an amoebic infestation. They lie dormant until in contact with fluid such as rain in the monsoon season. Unfortunately in this case it was the fluid of this young fella's eyes."

Cleaning away some of the fluid streaming from Eddie's eyes, the surgeon turned to the waiting Corporal. At rigid attention, the elder Mannock could not hide his worry and fear.

"Sir, er, will he see again? I mean, it's just a bug in his eye, isn't it?"

"In these cases we can't be certain. The right eye will almost certainly recover. The left one, I'm afraid, is another matter altogether. The cornea has already been damaged. How far that damage will spread or to what extent it will impair his vision, we cannot tell."

Within a fortnight the sight of Edward's right eye had returned to normal, and the left was improving daily. Although the pain had continued throughout, his greatest pain came from the vicious reaction of his father to the illness. He was constantly bombarded with cutting comments: he was no proper Mannock; he would never be a whole man and hold down a man's job; he would get nowhere reading his 'daft' books about things better left to women and girls. At the age of ten, Eddie was unaware of the older man's true feelings. Corporal Mannock looked on his son's affliction as a question upon his own manhood and, even after the boy's sight returned to near normal, would treat him so badly that he would never take back the hate he felt for his brutal father. This conflict between them would, however, have a positive effect on the development of Edward's character.

Often threatened with his father's raised fist or boot, Edward discovered the power of courage. When faced with a brutal beating, he found it was best to show courage rather than depend on the protection of his mother. Instead of staying behind her when she intervened, he would step forward and face the raging Corporal, his chin stuck out proudly. Courage, he concluded, even sham courage, could help one out of the most terrifying situations. This was a lesson he would put to good use throughout the years to come.

In 1898 the South African war took Corporal Mannock's regiment overseas for three years, but his long absence proved to be no great loss to Julia and her children. During their five years in India he had steadily moved back towards his former ways, the Army and his drinking friends replacing his family at the head of his list of priorities. So empty had Julia's life become that she too had taken to the bottle, but with the removal of the Corporal's suppressive presence, she once again returned to a normal life and her children. Edward was again under her influence, although this time she was only interested in the education he so desperately wanted.

At the end of the Boer War, Mannock returned with his regiment to Shorncliffe in England and sent for his wife and children, who joined him later at the Cavalry Depot in Canterbury. As in the past, absence had made his heart grow fonder, and the family was happy for a while. Within two months of his return, Mannock was released from service, and the old process began of looking for a job which would fill his life to the same extent as the army. The old campaigner found it hard going, leaving home every morning only to return downhearted and disillusioned. Two months after their reunion, Julia awoke to find her husband and their paltry savings gone. Tears and wailing could be heard from the Mannock household in Military Road for the next few days—none of the neighbours, however, were ever told of the Corporal's desertion. Julia rapidly recovered from her grief and looked to their future. She found a new home for them and drew the family together in an unbreakable bond; they would want for nothing if they held together for each other. Patrick had already started working with the National Telephone Company in Canterbury, and Jessie was able to pick up odd jobs from time to time. Edward, a pupil at St Thomas's was removed from school to assist in the family's upkeep. Refusing to join his brother in the stuffy atmosphere of an office, he found employment with a local greengrocer who paid him 2s 6d a week. Up to twelve hours a day were spent dragging heavy bags of vegetables from the basement to the front shop. Forcing his lean body around the shop, Eddie looked a pitiful sight in his patched clothes and much-repaired shoes. Julia found it difficult to hold back her tears as he returned on a Saturday evening, his tired face glowing as he handed over the pittance he had earned. Had she known her son better, she would have had no cause for worry.

As in India, Edward had found a goal and developed the drive to achieve his ends. This drive was increased by the family's poverty, for more than ever he had a reason to improve himself and 'become something'. He looked at each problem as a further step in the path that he must take, turning each depressing factor in his life into an uplifting and unbeatable force which drove him on. He had to hang on and find that 'something' which awaited him; what it would be, he had no idea.

A reputation for hard work and honesty assisted him in finding a job with the neighbourhood barber at twice his previous pay. Although this work was not technically difficult, the barber's customers never gave him a moment's rest, and he spent every moment running out for papers, cigarettes and beer, lathering unending rows of chins. Eddie gritted his teeth and carried on. His hard work earned him a favourable response from his boss, who allowed him time off to play cricket, his latest passion. He had watched the St Gregory's team during an afternoon spent in a nearby public park. Fascinated by the game, he had stepped forward and offered to take the place of a missing member. Asked if he had played before, he lied and answered that he was a bit out of practice but would soon get his hand in. The trouble with his eyesight had almost been forgotten until his first attempt at cricket showed that the weakened left eye could be a handicap. His first ball went wide of the wicket, but this was excused by his new companions. The second miss brought forth cat-calls and a number of cutting comments. He ignored the cries of the other boys to 'get off' and carried on regardless. Quickly his good right eye registered where the ball was actually going and how his attempts at correction affected its path. Luckily the impatient lads resisted the temptation to throw the 'duffer' off the field and allowed him the time to correct his aim. Around the tenth attempt, Eddie squared up to the wicket, ran and let fly. Straight and true the ball flew towards the batsman and with a loud click sailed off into the blue. To his fellow players, his elation at this common event in cricket was totally baffling. He sprang into the air waving and whooping like a Red Indian. As long as they knew Edward, he would never mention the meaning of that day, but since he was considered a bit odd, in the nicest sense of the word, they put it down to that. His reputation as a 'mad old Irishman' was being formed.

Apart from his regular visits to the cricket park, Edward tended to be a bit of a loner. Life at home was as good as could be expected in the circumstances, although there were pressures which he considered most annoying. Patrick had joined ranks with Julia to push Edward into a job at the telephone office. Jessie was up to something or other which he did not understand properly, for it came to his attention only through the long and violent arguments

she had with Julia. He longed for peace and quiet, some-
where where he could think and not be disturbed by the
interruptions of others. His love of nature had led him into
fishing, from which he derived a great amount of satisfaction, not to mention a large number of poached fish with
which to feed the family. But fishing did not satisfy all his
needs. He desired civilized debate and company. By the
time he was fifteen years old, he was already becoming
slightly intolerant of his family and their way of life. Any
debate would soon become an insult-throwing match in
their hands; only Paddy had any sense when it came to
talking, although he was not really interested in matters
other than his job.

In 1903 Edward met Mr Cuthbert Gardner, a Canterbury solicitor who ran the local branch of the Church Lads'
Brigade and who invited the Catholic Mannock to join this
Protestant organization. He was thrilled: trips into the
country for weekend camps, debating clubs, meeting
people who were interested in 'things'. Julia's initial
religious opposition to the Brigade soon melted under
Edward's volley of enthusiasm. He threw himself into the
group activities in all possible ways and developed his
passion for music by becoming the brigade band
kettledrummer, a job which he undertook with much
energy.

Perhaps it was because of this partial relief from the
suppressive atmosphere of the Mannock household that
Edward suddenly submitted to his brother's request that
he join the staff of the telephone company. He had some
freedom and felt it only right that he contribute more to
the family income whilst releasing himself from their
constant nagging. Patrick's office colleagues welcomed the
new member to their ranks and made him feel at home as
much as possible. Initially the office seemed interesting
when compared with the repetitive routine of the
greengrocer and the barber, but the new skills he could
learn with the company were too few in number to satisfy
Edward's desire for that 'something'. After three years,

during which his health was affected by the indoor work, he requested and received a transfer to the engineering department of the company. Paddy was in no way pleased with his younger brother's desire to join the lower ranks of the firm, the labourers, but Eddie was pleased with his change. Apart from the fact that the work would interest his enquiring mind, he would have chances to get on and, most importantly, to leave home for pastures new.

Sad he might have been at the leaving of so many good friends in Canterbury, but this sadness was left behind more easily in the belief that he was on the next rung of the ladder that would lead to his 'something'.

Arriving in Wellingborough in the late spring of 1911, Edward started his new work enthusiastically. Climbing telegraph-poles, twisting and cutting the tough wires, out in all weathers, he loved the life and his new challenge. The 'digs' in Eastfield were not to his liking, full of rough types who kept him awake through the night with their drinking and singing, but life was good, and he had his diversions. In order to keep in touch with some of his friends from Canterbury, he had joined the RAMC (Territorial) before leaving home, which allowed him to meet them at annual camps, which he attended regularly. When he noticed an item in the local paper concerning a cricket match, he decided to attend and in so doing approached one of the most important crossroads of his life.

It was one of those picture-postcard days which foreigners look upon as the typically English scene. The bright, kindly sun shone down, warming the green grass and the trees which bordered its edges. Men dressed in baggy white trousers, white shirts and oversized sweaters stood casually around the cricket pavilion talking to delicately finished ladies. Engrossed in their chatter, beer-glasses held against chests, none of this assembly noticed the rather ragged youth with his slightly stooped, angular frame lumbering across the green. Edward tossed his old tweed jacket over one shoulder and looked about him for a friendly face. He felt slightly out of place amongst these well-tailored sportsmen—not even St Gregory's went into the game to this extent. Eventually finding a place beside a pleasant-looking man, Edward fell into conversation. His love for the game and his knowledgeable comments soon involved him in a long talk over a cold beer. The man introduced himself as A. E. Eyles but asked Edward to call him Jim. Many years later, Jim Eyles was to write of this day:

I first met Pat, as he was then known, about 1911 at a cricket match in Wellingborough. I was suffering from a rather painful boil on the side of my neck and, during our initial talk, asked him to stand in for me. After scoring nil, I think, he came over to apologise, and we fell into a long conversation. I was impressed with him immediately. He was a clean-cut young man, although not what one would call well dressed; in fact, he was a bit threadbare. We talked about his digs and it was obvious that he was not happy with this place. I asked him if he would like to move in with my wife and myself, and he was most happy about the idea.

After he moved in, our home was never the same again, our normally quiet life gone forever. It was wonderful really. He would talk into the early hours of the morning if you let him—all sorts of subjects: politics, society, you name it and he was interested. It was clear from the outset that he was a Socialist, but not in the sense of today. He was also deeply patriotic and would flare at the least suggestion of anything anti-British or anti-Crown.

I felt that he was in a home he could call his own for the first time. He came out of his shell because he felt safe with us. He knew that he could air his ideas and not have them thrown back in his face. Some of his concepts were a bit confused due to his rather sketchy self-education, so he really needed to talk them over and put everything into perspective. With all honesty, I can say that Pat developed while he was with us. We gave him the exercise-ground he needed, and it was good to see him grow. He was constantly on the move mentally, his confidence grew, and then he was looking for something else to pose a challenge. He lived as if he had but a few years of life and had to make something out of his time that would make it all worth while. How true that would be, and how well he did it! The drive for it all came from the years of pain with his family, I am sure of that. One could see the change in his eyes that came when he spoke of those early years. His hate of it all made him run towards some ideal that only he could see. He knew that there was something inside him, and he wasted no time in finding it. There was something different about him, a quality which held everyone he came in contact with. Most of the great men in history have had that something special in one form or another. It was not mere ambition, because he was incapable of the cold ruthlessness that one finds in ambitious men; a kinder, more thoughtful man you could never meet.

Nightly debates with Eyles and his wife helped Edward to piece together his confused collection of facts and ideas into a more rational and organized philosophy. He made full use of the books which filled the Eyles home—history, philosophy, great literary works, all were consumed greedily.

Edward also developed his musical talents at this time. Mrs Eyles was an accomplished pianist and encouraged him to try difficult pieces. He spent many hours with her in the front room by the piano. The old violin, the only gift he ever received from his father, held gently in his long bony fingers, he would struggle with the works of Mozart, Bach and Schumann. Although he would never learn to read music, Mrs Eyles coached him until he had mastered the pieces with sufficient skill to encourage him to further efforts. Singing also became one of his favourite pastimes. He became a welcome 'turn' at the social evenings held weekly by the Eyles, standing slightly embarrassed behind the piano, his rich baritone voice flowing over his favourite songs. Most of his friends of that period remembered his emotional renderings of 'Danny Boy' and more serious pieces from the *Faust* opera by Gounod. So impressed was Mrs Eyles with his singing that she introduced him to Madame Novello while on a trip to London.

He was accepted by this highly acclaimed mother of the famous composer and managed to take a number of singing-lessons from her before his other activities ruled them out. In this atmosphere of friendly comradeship, Edward could not help but grow into maturity. The friendships formed in Wellingborough, and those formed in artistic and academic circles, lifted his confidence to a previously undreamed-of level. He was surprised to the extent at which he, Eddie Mannock, the little army brat dragged up in the most awful squalor, could match wits with these high-born and well educated classes.

Jim Eyles again:

Pat and I had grown very close, like brothers or even father and son. But it did not take this close a relationship for me to see that he was now ready for a stage in his life which we could not help with. He was by this time, around the end of 1913, supremely confident in his abilities to take on the world. The world was growing; a new age was just around the corner. We all felt this, but none so acutely as Pat. He was more than ready to take his place in the world, the place for which he had worked so hard and deserved so much. He told everyone he met that everyman should prepare himself for the new age. The downtrodden of the world were about to get their chance at last; it was a duty for men to make the best of this opportunity for which the up-and-coming leaders of the new ideas (he admired Keir Hardie, H. G. Wells and the Fabians) had suffered so much. He became restless again, to an even greater extent that he had been when we first met; something was going to happen, and we did not have long to wait. One morning, at breakfast, he leaned across, looked me straight in the eye and said,

"Jim, I must go abroad. Not too sure where just yet, but will you help me? I don't have much in the way of savings, so I would have to pay you back once I'm settled."

This rather embarrassed him, having to borrow from me, but I soon put his mind at rest. My wife and I talked it over and agreed to lend him whatever he needed. He was over the moon when we told him, and he settled down to making decisions as to where he would go. He considered plantations and mining-operations in various parts of the world—in Africa and the West Indies, I believe, but through friends at work he heard of a cable-laying operation in Turkey and settled for that. He walked around for weeks with that glint that he always had in his eye when he was up to some devilment or when he had come up with some good idea; I could see easily that he was ready for whatever might happen. When he walked out of our little home in Mill Road, I knew instinctively that he was off to something great.

The parting took place on 9th February 1914. Little did Eyles know that Edward was leaving without first securing a position in Turkey. He wanted some adventure in his life. If the Turkish idea fell through, he would move on until something else came up. In Europe, the 'Guns of August' were gathering, but for Edward Mannock life would temporarily be full of smaller, more urgent matters.

The streets of Constantinople shocked him to his core. Everywhere he looked, there was filth and squalor; children who reminded him of himself and the thousands he had seen in India thronged the streets begging for food and money. He felt slightly guilty about the gold sovereigns hidden in his walking-stick, a present from friends in Wellingborough. Throwing the last of his change to a group of ragged beggars, he set off to find the office of the 'Société Ottomane des Telephones'.

2
The Motive and the Means

"Good morning Sir, my name is Edward Mannock"—he had practised that line again and again. At the signal from the secretary that her boss was ready to see him, he had taken an enormous breath, and now he strode into the small office, blurting out the words with as much confidence as he could muster.

"Ah, yes, Mr Mannock, you are looking for employment with the Company, I hear. Done this sort of work before, have you?" Edward leaned back in his chair and continued with suppressed nervousness, "Oh yes, worked with the Company in England, rigging lines and repairs. Just thought I'd pop out here to see what was available in Turkey. I fancy a move." Taken slightly by surprise, the manager leaned forward, his eyes wide with question, "You just packed up in England and sailed out here without finding a job. Why didn't you apply through the head office. All very adventurous, I admit. You must have money to spare, I take it." "Not much to speak of, just enough for a few weeks. If I'd gone through channels, my application would only just have reached your desk, and you would still have no idea of what I'm like."

After asking a few questions to check Edward's knowledge of the job, the most impressed manager hired him on the spot. Edward wrote home to Eyles: "No more climbing irons for me! Diagrams and a blue pencil! I have been using my head out here."

The letter conveyed his enthusiasm and happiness in success but it told nothing of the hardships and problems he was experiencing. Given the task of supervising Tur-

kish labour, Edward was faced with the hatred of the
Turks for the British, the non-productive nature of the
natives, to say nothing of the cruel and barren terrain.
Every day was a long, hard struggle to keep the men at
work, using his wits and charm to push them on. Feeling
lonely and extremely homesick, he wrote home: "How I
long sometimes to have a night with you and the old piano.
Not much opportunity for a good song and accompanist"
(sic).

Dedicated work brought results which put him on a good
footing with the company. One by one the new exchanges
were commissioned and lines laid. Edward, forced to mix
with the English community of Constantinople for much-
needed companionship, kept his distance as much as possible. Surrounded by the pretty daughters of diplomats, he
put his advancement first and avoided any affairs. One
girl (her name is unknown) is rumoured to have become
close to him, but only in the way he would allow. She
seemingly had the ability to converse on a higher level
than was normal amongst the unemancipated women of
the time, and he found her a joy to be with, a pleasant relief
from the strains of his work and a reminder of home. She
and Edward would discuss the world around them and one
of the main topics was the possibility of war in Europe. He
had for some time been aware of potential German aggression and had argued long and loud with those who refused
to see the irrefutable facts.

The murder of Archduke Ferdinand and his wife, the
Duchess of Hohenburg, on 28th June 1914, finally convinced Edward that a conflict of enormous proportions was
about to begin.

On August 4th 1914 he was standing beside his female
friend on a croquet court when news of Britain's declara-
tion of war came through. Britain, France and Russia were
standing together against the massive German war-
machine, which few believed could be stopped. Turkey was
being courted by the Germans with money and the prom-
ise of an enlarged Turkish empire. Enver Pasha, the pro-

Prussian leader of the Turks, wavered on the brink of war, unable to weigh up the pros and cons of joining one side or the other. His delay in making this decision ensured that Edward and his companions were trapped in Turkey. Like all the foreigners in the country, they could only wait and see what fate and the Germans had in store. They had but six days to wait.

Ordered to interfere with the British trade-routes to and from the Suez Canal, the German navy sent the ships *Goeben* and *Breslau* to handle the task. While off the Dardanelles, the German ships spotted what they thought was a Royal Navy squadron steaming towards them. This 'squadron' was in fact only one ship, HMS *Gloucester*, but the Germans' mistaken identification caused the *Goeben*'s captain to break for the Dardanelles, followed by the *Breslau*. HMS *Gloucester* gave chase at full speed and succeeded in hitting the German vessels, causing minor damage to their superstructures, but 11-inch shells from the German guns forced the Royal Navy to retire and allow the enemy to reach safety of Turkey waters. On landing, the German sailors were treated as heroes by the Turks: huge crowds turned out to greet them at the harbour, banquets were arranged in their honour, and the Sultan gave a special audience to one of the captains. Edward and the foreign nationals watched the proceedings with a mixture of hate and anticipation. What would happen next, they could not tell. Edward left the quayside and prepared for the worst.

Within twenty-four hours of the *Gloucester*'s reporting her contact with the German raiders, the British representative, Sir Lewis Mallet, and his colleagues from the free nations delivered an ultimatum to the Turks. This demanded that the German vessels must either depart from Turkish waters or be interned. Enver Pasha would now have to turn his back on one side or the other, Germany or the Allies. Berlin came to his aid once more by advising him to inform the British that Turkey had bought the *Goeben* and *Breslau* and that they were now

Turkish property. This ruse was believed by many, but Edward knew the Turks and could see the German influence in this tactic; he knew that the Turks were incapable of such invention. Impatiently he waited for some advance in the situation.

Weeks of waiting for the Turks and the Germans to cease their bargaining followed; the months rolled by. Edward's company continued to fulfil their contract with the Turkish government, although the now radically anti-British Turks did everything in their power to hold up the work. Working on the project, sometimes labouring himself in the absence of local workers, Edward steeped himself in the job. He found the waiting nerve-wracking and hoped for news—whatever it was and however bad it might be.

November 1914 saw the departure of Sir Lewis Mallet and his staff. The Germans had now almost complete control in the country, and Edward and his companions were declared prisoners of war. At first the Turks could not decide what to do with their British captives. Some wanted the POWs thrown out of the country; others called for the completion of the telephone network, and others demanded that they be incarcerated. Two days after the departure of Mallet, Edward and his friends were arrested.

He tried to keep their spirits up by leading the singing of patriotic songs and by 'ragging' the guards, but on arrival at the prison, he had his first bitter taste of the Turkish penal system, one which had not seen reform for centuries. Men and women were forced to strip in the same room while the guards leered at the younger women and girls. Possessions were thrown on the floor, any attempt to recover these items ending in their loss. Edward held his walking-stick and pretended that he needed it as a walking-aid.

Separated from their wives and daughters, the men began to panic at the thought of what might be happening to them at the hands of the Turkish guards. Screams and struggles had been heard from the young women in the adjoining block, and after several hours rumours of rapes and beatings started to filter through to the male quarters. Edward continued his attempts at maintaining morale throughout, but even he began to flag under the harsh conditions. Hours of singing and kicking the communal cell door had taken its toll of his energy. Trying desperately to stay awake, he pleaded with the other men to continue the singing and harassment of the guards. Then a rumour, handed down from the main gate, tore him from his semi-conscious state. The Turks had planned to deport the foreigners, but this decision had been reversed by the Germans. Edward could not contain his fury. Banging on the heavy metal door, he shouted all manner of insults at any German within earshot. He had long considered the Germans a threat to civilization, and now he had seen them at their worst.

After several attempts at sabotage and escape, Edward was transferred with a number of other men to a concentration camp outside the city. Life was hard for the prisoners in these camps; food handed in for the inmates was stolen by the guards; conditions were appalling and punishment was severe. Knowing that Mannock was a 'flag-waver', the guards singled him out for special treatment. He would be tripped as he carried some watery rations back to the infirm; he would be insulted and kicked. Refusing to be drawn by his captors' jibes that "England finished . . . King's Mother a whore", Edward replied by thumbing his nose or by returning the insults with a gentle and seemingly complimentary tone. Although growing weak, his strength was reinforced by the growing hatred he felt towards his captors and especially their German allies. He could not stop the beatings and other cruelties, but he could and would do something about the lack of food. During a visit from a friendly Turk who had worked for him, he arranged for help with a plan to feed his starving companions.

In the early hours of the following morning, the long

frame of Eddie Mannock eased out of a narrow window and dropped to the ground below. He stopped for an instant to check his surroundings and then made towards the wire compound fence in a crouching run. On reaching the wire, he lay still and listened for the presence of guards. At any moment he could expect to be shot without warning; he braced himself and began cutting through the heavy barbed wire. Each of the wires parted with a crack which he felt must be heard by the guards. His nerves pulled as tight as the wires with each snap of the pliers. As the last length parted, he threw a quick glance towards the guard-hut and then sprang towards the nearest cover.

Two hours later he was back in the barracks, sharing out the heavy bag of food supplied by his friend Ali Hamid Bey. Edward was given many pats on the back for his kindness, but the trip had greater meaning for him than the provision of food. He felt good at being able to fight back instead of letting the 'Huns' have it all their own way. Realizing that he might never be able to return and join up with the forces in England, he continued his food-finding trips and planned other schemes against the enemy.

After a number of successful trips out of the camp, Edward set out one night unaware that he would return to a trap. While he sat with Ali Bey, the Turks had dis-covered his exit-hole and placed a guard on it in case the escapee should return. Return he did, only to be greeted with the point of a long bayonet. He was pulled from the hole in the fence and pushed along by the butt of a rifle towards a small concrete box which stood in the centre of the camp compound. Solitary! He breathed a sigh of relief, for he had expected to be shot.

The solitary-confinement 'cage' in this prison was in-deed a 'hell-hole'. He was locked in a concrete box far too small to accommodate his 6-foot frame, and he could not sleep with any comfort. His already weakened body be-came covered in open sores which oozed and refused to heal. Dysentery racked his intestines and made the con-fines of the cell even more unbearable. His previous subtle comments turned to undeniable insults, his descriptions of the enemy and his parodies of popular songs becoming even more direct and at times quite obscene. Two weeks of this treatment turned Edward Mannock into an inferno of hate. Daily, when the guards came to hand over his punishment rations, he would grab the greasy bowl from their hands and quickly shout a few insults through the tiny door hatch before it was closed up. The sunlight which beamed into the dark hole was painful to his eyes, but still it felt good. The pain which racked his head after these brief exposures to the life-giving rays was forgotten when he thought of the trouble he was causing the Turks. It may not have helped the war effort in any way, what mattered was that the other prisoners might be encouraged to do likewise. Long after the sun had gone down, those others would still hear his call: "Damn the sodding Huns, Bloody Huns."

Edward had long forgotten what day of the week it might be when his bleak world was illuminated by a long flash of brilliant light. The pain in his eyes was unbearable, each socket feeling as if it had been burned clean of flesh. Through his screams he could hear a strange voice— not a Turkish voice but American. Choking back his tears, he crawled to the small doorway and through squinted eyes tried to see who had come to help him, for surely this must mean help. A loud noise inside his head prevented his hearing the entire conversation, only a few words of that delicious accent filtering through to his straining ears. Questions were being asked about his health and the length of time he had been held in the filthy cage. The rest of the questions faded away as he found himself being dragged away by the shoulders.

As his eyes slowly opened some hours later, Edward sensed that he was being watched. The blurred figures of two people were standing over him and calling his name. As consciousness returned, he began to understand what the American was trying to say. He was to be repatriated along with others but would have to wait his turn while the more serious cases were being sent home. He wondered what the more serious cases must be like if they were in a worse state than himself. Desperately needing rest, he nodded his understanding and fell back slowly to the hard mattress. Two months later, he was one of many being herded onto a steamer bound for England.

This last leg of the journey would be the most difficult for his now fragile health. Weeks of travel through Bulgaria and Greece had nearly finished him, a recurrence of malaria contracted in India returning to aggravate the conditions which still persisted from time to time in Turkish hands. Doctors attending the sick passengers had tried to comfort him with the fact that he would be useless to the war effort and could have a quiet time during the coming months of conflict. Edward's answer, that he wanted to get into the army and "kill as many of the swine as possible", was dismissed as the rantings of a desperately sick man. He would recover in time, they thought, once the memory of his harsh treatment had gone. The doctors might have changed their professional opinion had they been witness to his first actions on returning home.

No one took much interest in the tall, ragged figure as he walked the streets of Canterbury and Wellingborough. Life-long friends passed him in the street and failed to recognize this scarecrow figure as Eddie Mannock. Set deep in his drawn and sallow face, Edward's burning eyes stared straight ahead, every ounce of energy being necessary to keep him on his feet and moving. As his friends and family opened their doors, they could not help but show their shock and horror at his dreadful state. For the first time in almost a year, he allowed himself to relax. Forcing a smile from his pale lips, he assured each of them that he was in the best of health and that his appearance was deceptive. But to none of them did he tell of his experiences, his now consuming hatred for the Germans and their creed of war. Jim Eyles remembers him at this time:

He looked an absolute mess. His clothes were sizes too large for him, the sleeves covering his hands. He had lost a great deal of weight but explained this away by saying that it was good for him as he had gained too much 'beef' by over-eating in Turkey! As far as the war was concerned, he confined his comments about this to asking for the latest news and saying that he would go back eventually to the RAMC and try to do something of use. I knew at the time that he would not take the war so easily, for his hatred could not be concealed. When I told him of the most recent actions, especially the German gas-attacks, his blood ran hot. Even his waxy complexion could not conceal this. His face reddened, and I saw his knuckles going white as he clenched and unclenched them in a growing fury. He explained this away as being a 'blow off' of steam and laughed about an 'old crock' like him being in the trenches.

The following morning he looked more like the old Pat we had known, having dressed in his own clothes and cleaned up a bit. He picked at his breakfast, unable to eat, and then he said he had some business to take care of. I knew he was going to join up and took some comfort in the fact that at least the army would not take him in this state of health. He had, however, made his plans, and I could not have changed his mind in any way.

It was July 1915, and Edward Mannock was going to find his war. He had expected his move to active service to take place within weeks of his return, but it was not to be. His out-of-date papers posed the first of the many obstacles, but rather than sit around waiting for his recall, he forged ahead on his own, pushing every possible department for a speedy return to the service; no system of red tape had been invented which could stop him. To the military surgeons, who at this time could still afford to be choosy in their selections, he did not look like a likely candidate for the front, but he passed that obstacle with his usual measure of charm and persuasion. "Oh, I always look like this, always been on the thin side. Never felt fitter." He was back in the army with his old rank of sergeant, but his greatest troubles were about to begin, and from an unexpected direction.

From his first day in the unit Mannock could detect that something was wrong. The men lacked any kind of enthusiasm for the job in hand or for winning the war. He watched their half-hearted attempts during practice, their indifferent comments about each day's frightening news from the front. Always one to try to see the best in men, he decided that the fault lay in their lack of understanding and not with any lack of spirit or patriotism. He attempted to start a branch of the 'Wellingborough Parliament', a club he had organized before leaving for Turkey. He felt that discussion would bring out the right sort of attitude needed by his comrades. At first the response was feeble, most of the men stating that the idea was mad, but he persevered and in the end secured the support of the majority. Each man would represent a constituency and put forward his views as to the best way of winning the war. Many fine speeches were made, some of the most moving by Mannock himself, but he soon realized that they were only empty speeches. The men's attitude towards the war changed only slightly, and none appeared any more anxious to get to the front lines. It was all a game to them, he concluded, and to Eddie Mannock war was anything but a game. Maintaining his battle against apathy, he strove to find some other way of 'giving them a kick up the backside', but it was during a routine practice that he would find his own answer.

Kneeling over a civilian volunteer, Mannock demonstrated the methods of dressing various types of wounds. He emphasized the need for expertise as this work would have to be carried out under the most exacting of conditions when they got to the war. His lecture was punctuated with detailed descriptions of front-line dressing-stations—mud, filth, enemy bombardment, blood and mangled limbs. As the gory picture was formed in the minds of his students, a stronger mental image was forming in Mannock's fertile imagination. He saw himself in those horrific surroundings attending to some mutilated man, and it suddenly occurred to him that his patient might be a German. His mind's eye filled immediately with the image of a German soldier helped back to health under his own hands.

Mannock immediately applied for an interview with Major Chittenden, his Commanding Officer. Marching into the office with a purposeful stride, he put his case forward in no uncertain manner. Explaining that as a matter of conscience he could not spend the war tending the sick or driving an ambulance while his countrymen were dying in their thousands, he respectfully requested a transfer to the Royal Engineers as an officer cadet. Killing the enemy was the only way of winning the war, he explained, and that was what he wanted to do. Holding back his rising anger at this man who he felt to be an upstart, Major Chittenden agreed to forward the request for consideration.

Carrying out his duties day by day, Mannock waited impatiently for news of his transfer. Every call to the Commanding Officer's office would jar him into a highly excited state, but most of the summonses were routine and disappointing, and even news of his promotion to Sergeant Major did little to stop him brooding. But one morning in March 1916 was different. In his usual manner, Mannock arrived at the unit's office to check the bulletin board for the day's duty-notices. With a now practised eye, he ran down the lists of names and duties, not expecting the word which seemed as if it would never come. Running his finger down the typewritten lists, he suddenly came to an item which stood out for him like a flashing beacon: "Sergeant Major Mannock, E. RAMC, to Royal Engineers Signal Section, Fenny Stratford." He could not contain his happiness at the news. Running through the gathering of ranks of sleepy soldiers, he laughed at their puzzled faces and made for the adjutant's office to collect his travel papers.

However, Fenny Stratford afforded Mannock no relief from the apathetic world of the Wellingborough RAMC. His fellow officer candidates seemed interested mostly in their bright new uniforms and comparing the results of the never-ending examinations. Realizing that his sketchy education might bring about his downfall against these well educated companions, Mannock threw himself into the work without rest. His insular behaviour earned him the reputation of being 'a bit of an odd 'un'; he ignored the comments. The constant waiting brought about a small decline in his enthusiasm, a decline almost completed by the attitudes of his comrades. His energetic comments and questions about the war and what they all might achieve were directed towards deaf ears. Hardly able to believe it, Mannock listened daily to the banal conversations around him—the abilities of one military tailor compared with another, the clubs one could enter wearing an officer cadet uniform, how the girls of London flocked to the sight of a brave officer in his colourful plumes. Mannock's reputation grew as he regularly threw down his books and stormed away from these 'boys' playing at war. His hatred of these members of the ruling classes grew almost to match his hate of the Germans and secured his ostracization from the group. He realized that his failure to join the group might affect his chances of commission but decided that his dedication to the destruction of Germany was more important than the acceptance of others; he would get to the war without their sanction, one way or another.

Mannock's efforts at this time clearly indicate his fervent desire to engage the enemy, but for him the situation was not so simple. He hated the enemy, but at the same time he hated the British ruling classes—it was they, he felt, who would gain from the war. His deep patriotism won the argument. Life in Britain might be hard and unjust, but the Germans and their 'boorish *Kultur*' would forever destroy the chances of a free existence. During this period he searched his soul and suffered much mental anguish. He was a kind man who, under normal circumstances, would have found the idea of killing abhorrent. So began the conflict between the two sides of his nature, the naturally kind man and the killer through necessity in war.

Thoroughly depressed with his comrades' attitudes, Mannock decided to make full use of a ten-day leave. In Wellingborough he could put aside the uniform of a probationary Second Lieutenant and talk things out with Jim Eyles. A great believer in the power of conversation, he knew that Eyles would help him find the answers, but unknown to Mannock the answer would find him long before he reached home.

Ticket in hand, he paced the platform of Bedford railway station and let his thoughts flow under the hot June sun. Life at Fenny Stratford had taken its toll of his energies to such an extent that even he was beginning to doubt his beliefs, and so depressed had he become that even the horrible memory of Turkey had begun to recede into the far corners of his mind. Amongst his racing thoughts that day, only one idea held firm under the mental deluge: Turkey and everything he had seen there must not be forgotten. The memory of the beaten bodies, the starving faces, the molested women and the frightened children, all of these pictures flooded back to strengthen his resolve. He would get to the war and destroy the evil which had caused so much suffering. But how? His thoughts were disturbed by the face of an old friend who, on his left breast, carried the wings of the Royal Flying Corps.

Over a quick drink in a nearby hotel, Mannock ran over the past years for the benefit of his long-lost friend, Eric Tomkins. Describing the move he had made to Wellingborough, his face lit up with happiness, but once again it resumed its saturnine gaze as he went over the memory of Turkey for the second time in an hour. Frustration, he explained to Tomkins, was his main problem. Every move he had made towards getting nearer to the war had been swamped in one way or another. Tomkins suggested a move to the Flying Corps, a suggestion which he at once rejected. His age and physical condition, to say nothing of the fact that he had already belonged to two different units in under a year, would not, he felt, assure the Flying Corps of his reliability. Boarding his train, Mannock assured his friend that he would try to join him in the Corps, but in reality he felt that it would all be a waste of time. However, the seed which Tomkins had planted would soon start to grow.

Ten days later Mannock reported back for duty at Fenny Stratford—ten days in which he had thought long and hard over Tomkins's suggestion. Gathering together all the newspapers he could lay his hands on, he made a thorough search of their contents for news of the aerial war then being fought over the bloody fields of France. One man stood out for all to see, one which would always have a profound effect on Eddie Mannock: Albert Ball.

Ball had become the first of the British airmen to be given any publicity in the popular Press. The opinion of the British High Command was that to single out any one man for special praise was wrong and best left to the Germans and the French, but the heavy toll of the war, and the subsequent decline in civilian morale, had forced them to make public the names of the men who were scoring successes against the German hordes. Ball had captured the imagination of everyone in the country with his truly daring exploits. In his little Nieuport scout, he had taken on the élite of the German air service and scored against superior odds. Huddled in the tiny cockpit of his sleek silver machine, young Ball would dive down into the midst of a dozen or more Germans, shoot them to bits and fly off before the surviving enemy realized what had hit them. So good had he become at this deadly and dangerous game that his superiors had given him a roving commission to go where he pleased; individuality had to be allowed for in the air war.

His imagination fired by the stories of Ball's exploits, Mannock collected every piece written about the young Nottingham flyer. He read them time after time, one word standing out from the pages and drawing him to its meaning: individuality.

Since his time in Turkish hands, Mannock had considered in what way he might best be able to fight the Germans and had given much thought to improving the existing methods of human destruction. He had conceived the idea of placing tons of explosives under the impregnable German positions and blowing them 'sky high'. (This was used to great effect two years later at Messines Ridge in 1917.) He had thought of the brutal hand-to-hand fighting which took place between German and British tunnellers and wondered if he had what it took to withstand the pressures of this kind of warfare. Foremost in his mind had been the fact that he would be under orders from superior officers, some of them exactly like the apathetic types he had seen in the past. Not even his commission, which he wanted only for the independence of action he thought it would bring, could let him have full reign over his actions. But now there was this idea about flying and Albert Ball—individuality. That, he suddenly decided, was for him. In one little plane he could fight in a way suitable for him and not be under the eye of those "morons in brass uniforms".

In June 1916, Mannock was finally accepted as a fully fledged Second Lieutenant. Walking away from the cheering throngs of his equally successful fellow cadets, he bumped into Lieutenant Buchanan, his Commanding Officer, and decided to make his decision to transfer known. Buchanan stepped towards Edward, a smile on his face.

"Well done, Mannock. Now you can get on with that war of yours. I do hope that you will be all right and that. . . ."

"I'm going to apply for the Flying Corps, thought you'd better know."

Buchanan, an incredulous expression drawing across his face, took Mannock to one side and listened to his brief explanation. Two days later he received his written request for transfer and approved it, knowing that nothing he could say would change Mannock's mind.

14th August 1916 saw Mannock's arrival at the number

one School of Military Aeronautics in Reading, where he studied theory, maps, aircraft-rigging and gunnery. Although interested only in gunnery and the theory of flight, he passed with honours and was sent to Hendon for elementary flying instruction. On 28th November he was granted Aero Club Certificate Number 3895, and he was passed to No. 19 Training Squadron in Hounslow as a probationary flying officer on 5th December. He was then posted to the Hythe School of Gunnery on 1st February 1917 and spent two weeks there before moving on to No. 10 Reserve Squadron at Joyce Green for advanced training. According to his instructors, Mannock had a natural aptitude for flying and was happy and relaxed in the air. One of his instructors, Captain Chapman, remembered him as:

... a raw green 'Hun' (as we called the flying pupils under instruction) from Reading. I do not know, but he seemed not to have the slightest conception of an aeroplane. To do him justice, there were few wires which he did not loosen in climbing into the cockpit, but then the machine, a Henry Farman (or 'Rumpty' as they were commonly known), was at all times hard to get into. He finally managed to get into the pupil's seat, and we took off the ground. Mannock, unlike many pupils, instead of jamming the rudder and seizing the joystick in a herculean grip, looked over the side of the aeroplane at the earth, which was dropping rapidly away from him, with an expression which betrayed the mildest interest. I liked him immensely from that moment. He made his first solo flight with but a few hours' instruction, for he seemed to master the rudiments of flying with his first hour in the air and from then on threw the machine about as he pleased.

During his time at Joyce Green, Mannock met Captain James McCudden, who was on leave from the front and acting as a fighting-instructor. McCudden made a strong impression on Mannock and introduced him to the latest ideas in air fighting: team tactics and a more offensive use of the aeroplane. Mannock also made a strong impression on the instructor, as can be seen from a later prophetic writing of McCudden's: "The pupils here during the period of which I write were very good. One I particularly remember was named Mannock. Mannock was a typical example of the impetuous young Irishman, and I always thought he was of the type to do or die."[1]

A fellow pupil of Mannock's at Joyce Green was Captain Meredith Thomas:

> I first met 'Micky' in February of 1917 when he came along from Hythe to No. 10 Reserve Squadron at Joyce Green to fly DH2s and FE8s. We shared a room, and he told me many interesting stories of his pre-war life; it appeared to have been a hard one. At this time he was a staunch teetotaller and a fairly regular church-goer, although during chats with him he professed to have no particular religion.
>
> One particular incident regarding his flying training I well remember. That was his first solo on a DH2, when he was told, as we all were in those days, "Don't turn below 2,000 feet; if you do, you will spin and kill yourself." Micky proved this wrong one Sunday morning in March, when he accidentally got into a spin about 1,000 feet over the munitions factory—then just across the creek on the edge of the aerodrome—and came out extremely near the ground and the munition factory, and landed successfully in a small field which was too small to fly out from.

Mannock's 'accidental' spin was, in fact, intentional. He had taken the DH2 up on a routine practice flight and set himself the task of finding out exactly "what it would do".

At about 1,500 feet he eased forward the joystick and sent the machine towards the ground in a slow, shallow drive. Watching his height slipping away, he braced himself and waited for the magical figure of 1,000 feet to appear on the altimeter. Slowly pulling back on the throttle, he listened to the machine's motor descending to a purr. Timing his moves preciously, Mannock eased back on the stick and, as the motor reached its minimum re-

[1] From *Five Years in the Royal Flying Corps* by James McCudden VC.

volutions, pulled back hard. The de Havilland's nose pulled up sharply and then stood still in the air against the horizon. As the stalled machine slid backwards towards the earth, he steeled himself, for his actions during the next few seconds would mean life or death. The words he had memorized during a talk with Jimmy McCudden came back like lightning: "let her come out of the stall and centralize the controls. Once she is into the spin, apply opposite rudder, and as she slows down from the spin, ease the nose down." At the end of the stall, the machine flicked into the deadly spinning descent which had meant death for so many pilots. Mannock kicked hard on the rudder and waited for the end of the blurring which confused his vision. As the earth appeared clearly in front of him once again, he pushed forward on the stick which brought the aircraft back into normal flight.

Easing a sigh of jubilant relief, he adjusted the throttle for level flight and then saw to his horror that his trials were not yet over: 300 yards in front of him lay the Vickers munitions factory, hundreds of tons of high explosives and inflammable chemicals. Lacking the space and speed to climb away, he killed the engine and slammed the machine down hard, rolling to a halt only feet away from the factory wall.

After walking back from the stranded machine, Mannock was summoned to the Commanding Officer and 'carpeted' in no uncertain terms. Called all the irresponsible idiots of the day and threatened with being rejected for flying, he told one of the few lies of his life. He denied spinning intentionally and put the incident down to lack of experience. Walking away from the office building, he felt pleased with himself at disproving the DH2 legend, but this incident had had a greater significance for him. It set the pattern for his future development. During the months ahead he would be searching for the maximum capabilities of machines and men, especially himself, and determining a maximum level to which he could drive himself and his future followers. In this way he realized

early in his career that air combat was a science and not
the haphazard affair practised by many.

On 31st March 1917, his mind full of these high ideals,
Mannock sailed for France.

3
The First 'Kill'

The science of powered flight was still in its infancy when Edward Mannock arrived in war-torn France, but three years of bitter fighting had brought about great advances in design. From humble beginnings, the military aeroplane had been developed into a lethal and much respected weapon.

During the first months of the war, commanders on both sides had mistrusted the aeroplane, looking on it as usefuly only for scouting and of no great value as an offensive weapon. To the ageing generals, cavalry was still the answer to any military problem. Unaware of the carnage that would ensue from sending colourfully dressed horsemen against machine-guns and high-explosive shells, the belligerent nations embarked on a course which would cost thousands of lives before the folly of their outdated policies would be realized.

In the air, the war was carried on with an air of gentlemanly endeavour. The airmen of the time looked upon themselves as part of an exclusive club, an élite band of sportsmen whose activities had little to do with the nightmare of trench warfare being fought below them in the mud of France. Meeting over the lines in the early stages of the war, opposing airmen would simply wave to each other as they went their separate ways. This friendly respect between the flyers was not allowed to continue, however. Realizing the value of the aeroplane in directing artillery fire and spotting troop-movements, military commanders ordered flyers and ground forces to attack enemy machines and thereby deprive the enemy gunners of their 'eyes in the sky'.

By modern standards, the first attempts at fighting in the air were laughable, bricks, stones and even small articles of furniture being taken aloft as the first air-to-air projectiles. Weighted chains were thrown into the paths of enemy machines in order to damage their propellers; anchors were suspended on long ropes in attempts to damage vital parts of an opponent's machine. More logical and aggressive airmen began carrying firearms, and the science of air fighting entered its first truly lethal stage. While pilots struggled to hold their unwieldy machines steady, observers would stand up in their cockpits, usually surrounded by a maze of vital wires, and match shots with the enemy opposite-number. Some successes were achieved using these primitive methods, but it soon became obvious that more powerful weapons were needed.

Experiments using light machine-guns were carried out by flyers of all nations, but the first successful use of this weapon on a single-seat machine was achieved by a French pilot, Roland Garros. He and his colleagues realized that a forward-firing gun mounted in front of the pilot was the answer, and they set about perfecting a means of allowing bullets from the gun to pass through the propeller arc. They managed this by fitting small wedges of toughened steel to each blade and diverting the passage of those bullets which struck the blades. At the end of March 1915, Garros set off for the front lines in a Morane monoplane to test his device in action.

No pilot at that time had any reason to fear a tractor-type aircraft coming straight at him (the standard means of attack at that time being to fly in front of and on the same course as one's victim), and Garros therefore had the element of surprise on his side. Unsuspecting German airmen allowed him to fly directly behind them and realized their mistake only when it was too late. In sixteen days, the Frenchman and his little machine had accounted for five enemy aircraft—an unheard-of score at that time.

But his success was to be short-lived. On 18th April 1915 Garros was brought down by ground-fire while strafing troops, and his machine was captured intact. Realizing the value of this 'secret weapon', the Germans brought in Anthony Fokker to produce a copy of the arrangement. Within days, Fokker and his staff had discarded Garros's crude gear and developed an interrupter gear which allowed the gun to fire only when the propeller blades had passed out of the line of fire. This device was fitted to a Fokker monoplane and sent to the front for evaluation— the real air war was about to begin.

Flown initially by Immelmann and Boelcke, the Fokker proved vastly superior to any Allied type then at the front, and by the late autumn of 1915 the Germans had sufficient numbers of it at the front for it to be a real menace to the Allied air force. The period became known as 'the Fokker Scourge', the victims of the scourge as 'Fokker Fodder'. Flying their poorly armed BEs (Blériot Experimentals), Allied airmen were shot down by the score.

Not having an interrupter gear (although a design for one had been supplied to the British Government before the war), British aircraft designers set about finding an answer to the problem. Two aircraft were seen as being capable of opposing the Fokker, the DH2 and the FE2b, both pusher types. By mounting the engine and propeller behind the crew positions, a forward-firing gun could be fitted without the use of an interrupter. Sent to France, where they combined with the French Nieuports to regain aerial superiority, these machines overcame the Fokker menace and put an end to its invincible reputation by mid 1916. The race to find the ultimate fighter type was by no means over, however.

The German Albatros D1 fighter was a revolutionary design for the time. Apart from having a sleek, streamlined fuselage and powerful motor, it was fitted with two machine-guns firing through the propeller. The appearance of the D1 coincided with the reorganization of the German Air Service into *Jagdstaffeln* (hunting-squads) by Oswald Boelcke. The latter, who had survived the defeat of the Fokkers and scored many victories on the type, had developed the first true fighter tactics, using large, well trained flocks of fighters to attack specific targets in an organized manner. In order to ensure the continuing superiority of his force, Boelcke searched out the cream of the German pilots, and one of his selections was an unknown observation pilot called Manfred von Richthofen.

Meanwhile, the Allies had not been lax in their efforts. The mistakes of the past were being overcome; experts in the field of aviation were replacing the inexpert civil servants who had unwittingly deprived Allied airmen of suitable machines. Men such as 'Tommy' Sopwith, Fred Sigrist and H. P. Folland were coming to the fore, men whose creations would go down in the annals of aviation history.

By the spring of 1917 most of the gentlemen flyers of the early war years were dead. A new breed of men now ruled the skies over France, dedicated professionals whose only aim was to destroy as many of the enemy as possible. In the turmoil of a 1917 dog-fight, when dozens of aircraft were twisting and turning to latch on to the tail of their selected victims, there was no room for the sporting antics of the early flyers. The rule of the jungle had become the law of the air: stalk your prey and destroy him without mercy.

Unknown to Mannock, his arrival in France coincided with the start of the major German air offensive of the Great War, the battle that the British would forever re-member as 'Bloody April'. During that month of mass aerial destruction, the Royal Flying Corps would suffer at the hands of the Germans as they had never done before. Faced with the new German Albatros D3, which had been organized into 'circuses' by Manfred von Richthofen, the slow lumbering BEs and REs of the British would be massacred by the hundred, their obsolete fighter escorts unable to protect them. In Boulogne, the unblooded Second

Lieutenant Edward Mannock RFC opened his war diary
for the first time.

France, 1st April 1917
Just a year ago since I received my commission, and a year to
the day earlier I was released from a Turkish prison. Strange
how this date returns. Let's hope that a year hence the war
finishes and I return for a spell in Merrie England.
    Well, landed at Boulogne. Saw the MLO and discovered I
was to be away to St Omer the following day at 3.45 pip
emma. Rested and fed at the Hotel Maurice. Quite a nice
place as Continental hotels go. Wisher, Tyler and two more
strangers (RFC) kept us company. Rotten weather. Rain. I'm
not prepossessed with the charm of La Belle France yet.

After a few days of being moved around by officers who
had no idea what to do with him, Mannock received the
news he had waited for and noted in his diary.

6th April 1917
Ordered to proceed to 40 Squadron at a place called Aire,
Lens and Le Basses sector. Arrived at destination by tender
after 1½ hours' run. Cold, wet but cheerful. Met Captain
McKechnie and old Dunlop. Mess very nice and the Com-
manding Officer and Commander all that could be desired.
Posted to 'C' Flight-Lieutenant Todd, Commander.

This rather happy entry in his diary mentions nothing
of the somewhat cold reception which greeted Mannock on
his arrival at 40 Squadron. To a great extent, he bottled up
his true emotions, not even mentioning them in his private diary. The facts of his arrival at No. 40 were not so
pleasant.
    After reporting with his orders to the unit's adjutant,
Mannock met Major Leonard Tilney, the Commanding
Officer, and walked across the aerodrome with him to the
Squadron mess. Tilney explained the operations and func-
tions of the unit and outlined for Mannock the duties he
would be carrying out during his first days at the front.

Entering the mess, Tilney introduced him to Squadron members, most of whom had only just returned from a difficult mission. Attempting to cover his nervousness, Mannock made what can only be described as a mess of his first meeting with front-line airmen. Unknown to him, the flight had just returned from a meeting with some élite German flyers and had lost a well loved member of the Squadron. Lieutenant Pell had gone down out of control, and no hope could be held out for his survival. The atmosphere of the mess was heavy with grief at this loss, and Mannock's attitude, however innocent, was in no way appreciated. He committed the cardinal sin of asking each of the men about their personal scores against the enemy, put forward his own views about air fighting and the war in general and totally destroyed his first impressions by making his statements from the chair normally occupied by the dead Lieutenant Pell. Lieutenant Lionel Blaxland remembers Mannock's arrival:

He had had some training on pushers but had also had a lot of time on tractor rotaries, and it was hard for the men to see a new boy who had more time on the type than them. (We had only just converted from pusher FE8s at the time.) Apart from that, he was 'different'. His manner, speech and familiarity were not liked. He seemed too cocky for his experience, which was nil. His arrival at the unit was not the best way to start. New men usually took their time and listened to the more experienced hands; Mannock was the complete opposite. He offered ideas about everything: how the war was going, how it should be fought, the role of scout pilots, what was wrong or right with our machines. Most men in his position, by that I mean a man from his background and with his lack of fighting experience, would have shut up and earned their place in the mess. He seemed a boorish know-all, and we all felt that the quicker he got amongst the Huns the better; that would show him how little he knew.

On the following day Mannock flew the Nieuport scout for the first time and in the process had his first look at the lines. Having become accustomed to the rather heavy con-

Mannock in the uniform
of a sergeant, RAMC,
1915.

Mannock's aviator's
certificate, 1916.

Fédération Aéronautique Internationale
British Empire.

We the undersigned, | Nous soussignés
recognised by the | pouvoir sportif
F.A.I. as the | reconnu par la
sporting authority | F.A.I. pour l'
in the British Empire | Empire Britannique
certify that | certifions que
2nd Lieut.

Edward Mannock, R.E.

Born at Cork on the 24 May 1887,

having fulfilled all | ayant rempli toutes
the conditions stipulated | les conditions
by the F.A.I. has | imposées par la
been granted an | F.A.I.a été breveté

AVIATOR'S CERTIFICATE.   PILOTE - AVIATEUR.

THE ROYAL AERO CLUB OF THE UNITED KINGDOM.

_____ Chairman

_____ Ass't Secretary

Date 28 Nov. 1916. No 3895.

(Signature of Holder)

Opposite:
Mannock during training with the RFC, 1916.

Rook, McScotch, Crole and Davies at Bruay, 1917.

McScotch's Nieuport with twin Lewis guns.

Redler in a Nieuport 17.

Cudemore, Mannock, Hall and de Burgh (40 Squadron). This photograph was taken shortly after their balloon raid of 7th May 1917.

McElroy, Mannock's star pupil, with an SE5a, 40 Squadron, 1918.

Right to left: Kennedy, Godfrey and Blaxland and two friends.

Mannock in an SE5a D276, London Colney, April 1918.

Henry Hamer, 'Taffy' Jones and Lloyd Skeddon.

Lt H. G. 'Clem' Clements, 1918.

Lt 'Swazi' Howe, Lt Dolan and Capt Mannock

Lt W. B. 'Twist' Giles (*left*)
and Lt 'Taffy' Jones.

85 Squadron shortly before
Mannock became CO. *Left
to right*: Cushing
(adjutant), Dymond,
Daniel, Canning,
McGregor, Callaghan,
Springs, Horn, Randell,
Baker, Cunningham-Reid,
Longton, Rosie, Carruthers,
Inglis, Brown, Brewster,
uknown, Abbot and Dixon.

The party held by Mannock on the day before his death, 25th July 1918.
Above: second right, Lt D. C. Inglis; fourth left, Lt H. G. Clements.
Below: third left, Lt 'Taffy' Jones; far right, Lt D. C. Inglis.

Major Edward MANNOCK,
DSO (and two Bars), MC (and Bar),
No 85 Squadron, Royal Air Force

In recognition of bravery of the first order in aerial combat.
Major Mannock was credited with fifty victories, although his unofficial score was seventy-three. He was killed on 26th July, 1918, when shot down by ground fire.

Award promulgated 18th July, 1919.

The Mannock display in the VC gallery, RAF Museum, Hendon.

The memorial to Mannock in Canterbury Cathedral—note the incorrect date.

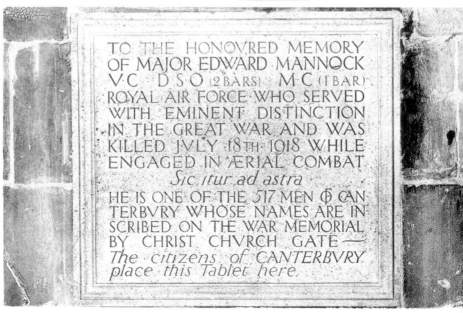

TO THE HONOVRED MEMORY
OF MAJOR EDWARD MANNOCK
V·C · D·S·O (2 BARS) · M·C (1 BAR)
ROYAL AIR FORCE WHO SERVED
WITH EMINENT DISTINCTION
IN THE GREAT WAR AND WAS
KILLED JVLY 18TH 1918 WHILE
ENGAGED IN ÆRIAL COMBAT
Sic itur ad astra
HE IS ONE OF THE 517 MEN Ð CAN-
TERBVRY WHOSE NAMES ARE IN-
SCRIBED ON THE WAR MEMORIAL
BY CHRIST CHVRCH GATE—
The citizens of CANTERBVRY
place this Tablet here.

trols of his machine, he turned east for a clear look at the war. Although he had used his vivid imagination to picture the scenes depicted in the Press, what he saw was a shock to him. Mile upon mile of barren landscape stretched out, the seemingly endless texture of raddled mud broken only by the network of trenches and shattered buildings. Only the flashes of the artillery served as a reminder that this scene was on the planet Earth and not on some distant dead world. Mannock settled into the Nieuport's snug cockpit and thanked fate for sparing him a life in the trenches. That first glimpse of the terrible war on the ground convinced him that his place was in the air.

Over the next few days he would follow the pattern set by hundreds of other neophytes, orientation trips to the front lines, formation flying and gunnery practice being his main pastimes. Mannock preferred to be in the air at this time for the attitude towards him in the mess was becoming increasingly cold. Although shunned to an extent, he still tried to join in the conversations and 'rags' which made up the main recreation of the pilots. A number of new comrades warmed to him after a time, finding his searching mind and various talents a refreshing change from the 'public school common-room' set-up of the mess. One of his first close companions was Lieutenant de Burgh, a fellow Irishman. Nightly they would discuss the Irish question fervently and finish off their entertainment with a friendly boxing-match—much to the annoyance of the other men in the mess. Tables were knocked over, and glasses flew in all directions as the two men rolled and ran about the small room.

It was during the debates with de Burgh that another member of the mess took an interest in Mannock. Lieutenant Bond had been a reporter with *The Times* before the war and was drawn by Mannock's cutting oratories and fiery philosophy. Most of the Squadron were insulted by his 'gutter politics', but Bond found them fascinating.

Practice firing at a stationary ground-target had convinced Mannock that he would be able to bring down the enemy with little experience of the real thing. In fact, his first combat was to shatter his hopes of success in the air and convince his comrades that he was useless for the job.

His diary relates his feelings in combat for the first time: *"13th April 1917. . . .* I went over the lines for the first time, escorting FEs. Formation of six machines altogether. Heavily 'Archied'. My feelings very funny." What Mannock describes as 'feelings very funny' is yet another example of the understatement he used in his diary and in conversation. On this day he had had his first taste of a sensation unknown to him, cold, unrelenting fear.

It had happened as the formation had crossed over to the German side of 'no man's land'. He had been nervous before, wrongly adjusting his motor, falling out of formation; this new sensation was something different however: a dryness which started at the lips and spread back to the arch of his throat, a trembling cold mass growing in the stomach, reaching down to his groin. The first violent burst of 'Archie'[1] had caused these sensations to shoot through his body, panic reigning supreme. He only recovered in time to rejoin the flight for the swift journey home. Subsequent patrols did nothing to abate this overwhelming fear.

Rumours began to circulate. Conversations in the mess would stop abruptly as he entered, the huddled groups of men in the corners facing away from his enquiring gaze. They had seen him in action, always the last to make a move; the least energetic flyer in the unit. To the seasoned fighters of 40 Squadron, any man who shunned combat was suspect, especially one who had breathed so much fire on his arrival. But on 19th April Mannock's critics would be forced to modify their opinion of him to an extent.

In his determination to succeed in the air and gain the respect of his comrades, he took up a routine of daily practice. Whenever his machine was available, he could be seen outside the hangars preparing for yet another flight.

[1] Anti-aircraft fire.

Laughing at what they considered his way of shamming keenness, the pilots and mechanics settled down on the grass to watch the timid efforts of this 'windy type'. The little Nieuport climbed steeply under Mannock's hand and then descended slowly to 2,000 feet. He lined the nose up with the white target circle which lay in the centre of the aerodrome. Gradual pressure on the stick forced the Nieuport down and increased the speed to over 100 miles an hour. A little more pressure and the scout was diving towards the ground at an incredibly steep angle. Attempting to remain scientific and observant during his dive, Mannock watched for any unnatural movements in the machine's planes, attempting to find the maximum safe diving-angle and speed of his machine; the next movement forward of the stick brought the answer. CRACK! Mannock looked in horror as the lower right wing twisted in its mounting-socket, folded back and then tore away to float through space. Veering sharply to port, the crippled aircraft headed for the earth at an increasingly deadly angle. His brain switched into high gear in an instant. Slamming down hard on the rudder bar and killing the motor, he fought to keep the machine straight while praying for the nose to come up. He pulled out with only feet to spare, holding the Nieuport in a slow glide until it settled lamely in a field near the aerodrome.

Running towards the crash, pilots and mechanics alike were relieved to see Mannock climbing from the crumpled scout. They watched him gesturing to the torn wing socket and shouting at his mechanic. He continued his criticism of the man until the others came running up towards him, but then, seeing that the old mechanic had had enough, he smiled and patted the grease-covered overalls and explained what had happened. It was not the mechanic's fault, he explained; slipshod construction had weakened the fixing, and the strain of the dive had completed the job. Apologizing for his 'little joke', Mannock headed back to the field muttering loudly about the greedy French manufacturers who made vast fortunes from supplying sub-

standard aircraft. Admitting that their newest member
had shown great courage and skill in landing his craft, the
men of 40 Squadron followed after him, although still of
the opinion that he was not 'the right type' for the job.

Hard and dedicated practice had failed to improve his
shooting; his bullets appeared to be hitting the target, but
later inspection showed that he had missed completely. He
would have sworn that his tracers were cutting up the
ground target, for he had seen them going in. Unaware
that many other pilots had suffered from this illusion,
Mannock set about finding an answer to the problem.

Climbing up on the step of his Nieuport, he examined
the adjustments fitted to the sights and the Lewis gun. He
would reset their angles and set them for accuracy at a
short range. If he got right up to a German and opened fire
from a short range, 20 or 30 yards, he could not miss. More
suppressed laughter could be heard from the men lying
about the field as Mannock had his aircraft pulled to the
firing-butts. Sitting on the edge of the cockpit, he could be
seen fiddling with the Lewis gun on the upper wing, the
sight on the front cowling, and then firing off a few shots.
On hearing the results from a bored mechanic, he went to
work again. He became obsessed with the sighting of his
guns, never allowing anyone to handle their service apart
from himself. His ammunition was carefully selected and
loaded before every mission, for in this way he would avoid
the frustration of losing a 'Hun' because of faulty bullets.

Practice followed each of his experiments on the now
shining scout. Diving repeatedly at the ground-target, he
adjusted his aim to match the speed and angle of descent,
letting forth a spray of bullets at the last moment and
pulling away when only feet from the ground. The once-
scattered shots were now becoming closely grouped and
moving nearer to the centre of the target with each
attempt. Success! However, his first attempts at using
these skills in action were not to prove so fortunate.

On the morning of 1st May Mannock took off from the
unit's new base at Bruay on an escort mission with the

other members of 'C' Flight. Watching the machine of
Captain Keen, his new flight commander, he could easily
keep his position and was able to relax. He had imagined
such a mission over and over again, fixing his planned
mode of operation firmly in his mind. He had decided that
an automatic reaction to circumstances would allow for
greater efficiency in battle, every ounce of energy being
directed towards the enemy and not the technicalities of
the job. Inhaling the cold air of his slipstream, he watched
the flight charge of four Sopwith 1½-strutters appear below his wing. Signalling to each other, the commanders of
both formations turned towards the line—their target:
Douai aerodrome, home of Manfred von Richthofen's
'Circus'.

As the scar of the front-line trenches slid under his wing,
Mannock decided to warm his Lewis gun by firing a few
rounds, standard practice in the Royal Flying Corps. Silence! Not one round would fire. Jammed solid. Fearing
the accusations of his comrades more than the prospect of
an unarmed patrol, he pressed on armed only with his
service revolver.

Hearing the sound of a distant machine-gun, he turned
to see a yellow and green aeroplane with large black
crosses diving on his tail. Fear and apprehension gave way
to aggression at the sight of the German. Mannock kicked
his machine round in a sharp banking turn towards the
German. A strange noise came over the sound of his
straining engine; seconds later he identified it as his own
screams of anger. The fact that the German could not
possibly hear him made no difference to Mannock; it
helped his nerves. Flying away from his charging
opponent, the German pilot made for Lieutenant Parry,
leaving Mannock to watch the scene. Captain Keen was
following an Albatros down as it cut a deadly track towards the Sopwiths, and Mannock saw the German pilot
riddled with bullets before he could reach the lumbering
two-seaters. As the enemy pilot went down from 12,000
feet, a Sopwith followed, trailing the ominous trail of

vaporizing petrol. Furious at himself for not being able to participate, Mannock glared at the swarming Germans, none of whom seemed willing to close with him. He returned to Bruay and wrote in his diary: "What is the good of it all?" He had but six days to wait for yet another example of wastage in war.

On 7th May, in the company of Lieutenants Scudamore, Hall, Redler and Parry and Captain Nixon, Mannock flew at a height of 15 feet on a balloon strike 5 miles behind the German lines. Major Tilney had evolved a new form of balloon attack, and this had been tested successfully on 5th April. It had, however, encouraged the Germans to take measures against 40 Squadron and their technique. As Mannock and his comrades flew through wave after wave of ground-fire, five Albatros D3s led by Lothar von Richthofen, brother of the famous Baron, were climbing into an attacking-position over the German balloon line.

Mannock watched Captain Nixon waving to each man in the flight and pointing out the particular balloon he should make for. Nixon waved Mannock towards a fat brown slug at the far end of the line. He pulled down his goggles and watched his target approach between the Nieuport's centre-section struts. While the members of the flight watched the imposing and highly dangerous balloons, Captain Nixon had peeled off unnoticed.

Like a swarm of wasps, the silver Nieuports arrowed towards their goals. Mannock watched each of the men in front of him fly into a wall of anti-aircraft fire and wondered if he was looking into hell. Tracer and explosive bullets, balls of fire which came roaring up like rockets, deafening explosions—all of these seemed to combine their efforts to increase his growing madness. He fought to ignore the flow of death passing his frail aeroplane and concentrated on the bulk of the balloon as it grew in his sights. At the last moment he sent off a long burst of tracers and then flew over the crumpling form of the balloon as it went down in flames. Putting his head down below the cockpit coaming, he put on full speed and ran for home. Had he looked to the north, he would have seen the falling remains of a broken aeroplane.

Seconds before the first Nieuport had opened fire on the balloons, Captain Nixon had made one last check of the sky above and spotted the German formation of von Richthofen. Knowing that his flight would be at an enormous disadvantage being below the enemy, Nixon peeled off and climbed to meet the diving Albatros. Hopelessly outnumbered, he fought desperately to protect his patrol, wheeling and diving amongst the gathering Germans. Lothar von Richthofen fixed on to the little Nieuport's tail and sent a burst of fire through Nixon's fuselage. He fell dead into the German lines; he had been with the squadron only two days. Back at Bruay, when Mannock heard the news of Nixon's brave sacrifice, he retired to comment in his diary:

Went over the lines from north of Arras to 5 miles behind the German trenches at a height of less than 15 feet, attacking Hun balloons. Six of us—Captain Nixon (missing), Hall, Scudamore, Redler, Parry and myself. All except the Captain returned safely with machines almost shot to pieces. Hall crashed on home aerodrome, as did Scudamore. Parry crashed just our side of the lines at the Canadian Headquarters. Redler crashed at Savy but returned here later and damaged his machine in landing. I was the only one to return properly to the aerodrome, and made a perfect landing. We all got our objectives. My fuselage had bullet holes in it, one very near my head, and the wings were more or less riddled. I don't want to go through such an experience again.

His sadness at the death of Captain Nixon grew stronger that evening with the arrival of a message from Headquarters. Albert Ball, the fiery boy who had inspired him, was dead, another victim of the von Richthofen 'Circus'.

Two days later, Mannock was alone on a voluntary patrol with Captain Keen, a third member of the flight having pulled out with engine trouble. At 16,000 feet over the German lines, Keen waggled his wings and pulled away to fly Westwards; Mannock continued towards enemy territory. He flew nervously into 'Hunland', constantly searching the sky for signs of enemy planes and the chance to test himself against an Albatros instead of a ground-target. Stiff from the effects of cold and the constant turning to scan his surroundings, he decided on one last look before turning for home. He examined the sky above the top wing, between the wings and below the bottom wing. Then he viewed the ground below and to the sides of his fuselage. Carrying on with the search, he moved round to check the tail and above to the rear.

About to turn back to his controls, something made Mannock stop and look again at one particular spot in the blue mass above him. There! Three dots, hardly visible against the glare of the sun, were diving rapidly onto his rear quarter. Gathering his racing thoughts, he evolved a plan. No use in running for home, for the enemy would cut him off before he reached safety and slaughter him. Only one solution, he thought: let them come down in the belief that he had not yet spotted them and then turn on them as they closed. Taking one last look to estimate the enemy's speed, Mannock relaxed his muscles and mentally ran over the movements upon which his life would soon depend: stick over sharply, top rudder, eye on the sight waiting for the first German to meet him as he came out of the banking turn. A nerve twitched in his back at the thought of the six machine-guns trained on him at that very moment. The Germans must be close; 100 yards, 50 yards. Now!

Mannock's highly tuned body reacted a split second before the first German fired into the air which he had been occupying. Looking up from his sights, the German pilot saw only the silver blur of the Nieuport turning out of his fire. Forcing his head forward against the pressure of his turn, Mannock glued his eye to the sight and lined up the first Albatros for a killing blow. The Germans were now turning also, and he had to drag the Nieuport around in its tight turn for another revolution, slowly bringing his sights to bear on the rearmost Hun. The crosshairs of the sight crawled along the image of the German in the Aldis sight until it reached a point just ahead of the enemy propeller. Mannock pressed his trigger but was met with silence. Once more the Lewis had jammed. Realizing his desperate position, he threw the machine into a spin and headed for the ground, all the time praying that the Germans would lose valuable seconds in locating him.

Pulling out of his diving spin, he gunned his motor, only to hear that other vital component splutter to a halt. Seeing the helpless target below them, the Germans lived up to their reputation of the time. Waving excitedly towards their floundering victim, they peeled off one by one and dived towards the weaving Nieuport. Mannock waited for them to pull out and then sent his machine falling in a spinning dive, the Germans following suit. Ignoring the constant hammering of the six blazing Spandau guns behind him, he squeezed himself into a small target and flew for his life, kicking his rudder from side to side, slipping out of the German sights and all the time heading for home. Due to the dead engine under his cowling, he was forced to lose height under the enemy, a bad mistake in air fighting, but speed was important and could be maintained only in this way. He huddled to an even smaller size and prayed for the firing to cease. After falling some 6,000 feet, he heard the German guns stop and turned to see his pursuers pulling back to the west. They had noticed the British lines, and the possibility of being hit by ground-fire had made him and his tiny plane seem unimportant.

So far from a suitable landing-ground, Mannock had to restart the dormant engine. By increasing his dive-angle, he coaxed the propeller into turning, at first slowly but then rapidly as the speed built up. One coughing cylinder fired and forced the rotary engine into greater efforts; others fired with a rough bark; then the complete set fired, and he once more had power. Rather than turn for home, he pushed open the throttle and headed for the German lines. Ten minutes of climbing through the clouds helped to settle his straining nerves, reaction to the shock of his escape making his hands unsteady on the control column.

Flying into a break in the cloud base, he spotted another enemy machine and only then remembered his jammed gun. Once more he turned the Nieuport for home, a flight which attacked his nerves with imaginings of German machine-guns rattling at his defenceless back.

Settling the Nieuport's wheels on the grassy surface of Bruay seemed an immense task to the trembling pilot. He undid his safety-belt and tried his utmost to control the tremors which now racked his body more than ever. As the plane rolled to a halt, he took a long, deep breath and sprang from the cockpit, only to be faced with the true extent of his fear. He felt as if the ground would no longer support his weight—it spun and shook beneath his feet, sending his stomach into spasms of nausea. There and then he decided to draft out of the air service; he would never be any use in this game and would tell Major Tilney so at the first opportunity.

"Get a Hun, did you, Sir?" Mannock looked sheepishly at the face of the smiling rigger and started to answer, only to change his words before they left his mouth. "No luck, damn it. Lewis jammed on the first round."

Hearing his own words, he decided that perhaps there was some hope for him. Something had made him cheer up in front of the rigger, perhaps something that might help him in the air. Major Tilney came forward to meet him. He needed no explanation of Mannock's feelings, for the long, gaunt face told him enough. Knowing that the weary pilot was due over the lines again within a matter of hours, Tilney decided to give him a rest and sent him to St Omer to pick up a spare aeroplane. Mannock nodded his acknowledgement and boarded an RE8 of 16 Squadron for the journey.

The ride in the RE8 gave him some privacy, a rare commodity on a front-line airfield. Sitting in the draughty rear seat, he went over the events of the flight and tried

desperately to understand his reactions. He had known
fear before in his life, but this had been different from any
of those previous experiences. It was a clinging fear which
stayed with him after the event which caused it was long
over. He knew that many pilots went home broken men,
their nerve gone completely. He had seen some of them in
Britain acting as instructors—broken, nervous wrecks,
who trembled and stuttered around the field. He could
accept becoming like that after months of war, but he had
been at the front for only a month, only hours of that time
having been spent near the enemy. Fear became the all-
consuming thought in his mind for the next few days as he
tried to understand its meaning and its solution.

Those days proved painful for Mannock, his confusion at
times making him wonder if he had gone mad. He had to
make a decision: to allow himself to run away and be sent
home in disgrace, or to stay and make the best of things.
He would force himself to fight and hope that he would live
long enough to 'learn the game'. His diary entries following his frightening experience on the 9th show a change in
his outlook and include some previously unseen comments
of a happy and even humorous nature.

13 May 1917 (Sunday), 12.15 pm
Lovely day again. Brilliant sun although we had rather sinis-
ter clouds and mist at 4.15 am. I was on the early-morning
line-patrol with Hall and New. Owing to the weather, we
decided to leave New behind (A 'New' Man), so Hall and I
started together at 4.45am. Hall got the wind up apparently
with the weather and returned at 5am. I went over the Lens-
Arras sector and amused myself with the clouds. Went
through a rainstorm over Arras. Quite enjoyable. The old
engine wasn't going very well. Met three triplanes and some
FE buses on the same route and threw a loop or two to show
there was no ill-feeling. No Huns to be seen—luckily for
them—as I felt rather blood-thirsty. Their 'Archie' gunners
upset my complacency somewhat for a while. Returned at
6.30am feeling as hungry as a flee [*sic*] on a china doll.
Hun came over here yesterday morning at 10am. Leaped

into the ether and gave chase, but he had to [*sic*] much start on me, being about 18,000 feet up. Chivvied him over his own lines.

Mannock's change of attitude brought about his gradual acceptance by the members of 40 Squadron. Drinks were handed to him in the mess by fellows who had previously shunned him. He was included in the trips into town which the Squadron made to let off steam during a break in the fighting. He had at last discovered the value of comradeship, that powerful bond which exists to such a great extent amongst men at war and which is generally misunderstood by non-combatants. Mannock sensed the change in his friends' reaction to him; it was not yet fully developed but strengthening day by day. His improved relations with the other pilots would help him through these first terrible months at the front. "*18th May 1917*. Went to Omer on 16th with Captain Gregory, Captain Keen, Bond, Jake (Parry), Thompson and Redler. Quite an exciting time, although I think I took a little too much champagne." Mannock was making friends, some greater than others, but the man with whom he would share his closest secrets and form a life-long relationship was only just arriving at the front.

Lieutenant MacLanachan, who joined 40 Squadron in May 1917, was to become a really close friend of Mannock's, so close that the book he wrote[2] and the letters which survive him provide some of the best insights into Mannock's character and especially his social life outside the Squadron. MacLanachan's first meeting with Mannock resulted in their immediate liking for each other.

McScotch (as Mannock was to christen MacLanachan) arrived from England straight from a course of flying under the famous Major Smith Barrie, a top flyer of the time. Anxious to see what this 'wonder boy' could do after his expert training, his new comrades did not even allow him to unpack. A Nieuport was dragged from the hangars,

[2]*Fighter Pilot* by McScotch (George Routledge & Sons).

and the confused pilot was supplied with a flying-helmet. McScotch climbed into the silver scout and prepared to show what he was capable of doing.

Over-anxious to make a good first impression, he made mistake after mistake, wrongly setting the sensitive engine-controls and thereby losing his motor power at 1,000 feet. This height being insufficient to start the Nieuport's engine in a dive, McScotch decided to make one last attempt at impressing his new comrades with one of his pet stunts, a spin. Easing back on the stick, he let the Nieuport slip into a gentle spin towards the earth. Without power, this manoeuvre was easily carried out, and he could relax as he headed down, confident of the hero's reception awaiting him below. At the last possible moment, McScotch turned the spinning machine into a glide and floated down for a perfect landing. A mechanic climbed up on the fuselage, and his expression came as a complete surprise to the happy pilot. He then realized the effect his spin had had on the spectators. At this time a spin was considered a lethal manoeuvre, one which should be used only as a last resort if a pilot found himself trapped by the enemy.

Walking across the field, McScotch was ignored by the other pilots, the Commanding Officer turning away from him and walking off the field. The pilot tried to apologize for his actions, but Major Tilney refused to listen. In his book *Fighter Pilot*, McScotch relates what happened next:

Muttering rebelliously to myself, I caught sight of a tall, weather-beaten pilot almost shaking with mirth. Anger nearly got the better of me; I glared at him until, nodding in the direction in which the Commanding Officer had disappeared, he said: "He hadn't much to say to you, had he?" Something in his healthy ruggedness arrested me. "No, it was a pretty miserable show, wasn't it?" I replied, wondering what devilment made this strange pilot laugh. "But why didn't he wait until I explained?"

"Because he was absolutely speechless. They all thought you were going 'plonk' to the ground. We don't like watching fellows kill themselves, and Tilney (the Commanding Officer), looked away when he thought you were finished." At this his laughter burst anew in hearty guffaws, and when these had subsided, he turned his searching blue eyes on me.

"Tell me, honour bright, did you shove her into that spin intentionally? I saw you kicking your rudder."

I told him it was a favourite stunt and asked: "Do you think he'll send me back for further instruction?"

"Not Pygmalion likely," he said emphatically. "Not when he knows you did it intentionally." Then, as an afterthought: "You pulled her out of it very nicely. If you can handle a machine like that, we want you in this squadron."

Ever afterwards I felt grateful to him for these friendly and encouraging words. They saved me my self-respect and at the same time showed me that he had a somewhat 'Puckish' sense of humour. In using 'not Pygmalion likely', he was bowing to authority which decreed that 'not bloody likely' was an unsuitable expression for an officers' mess as it was supposed to be in Bernard Shaw's play *Pygmalion*. His quick sight had enabled him to observe the movements of my rudder and, seeing the consternation and horror on the faces of the others, had caused him the keenest amusement. As we walked to the camp, little did either of us dream that this same sense of humour was to save our nerves on many later occasions.

"But that was a pretty dud show of handling an engine," I remarked. "I simply couldn't get the mixture once she was in the air." At this he looked serious. "I don't damned well wonder. That machine belongs to Jake Parry, and no one else in the Squadron will take her up. In any case, the old crock is going back to the depot. That's why they sent you up in her." He thought for a few seconds. "I've always told them they'll kill someone through sending fellows up on their first solo on the worst machine in the Squadron. That's what shook their insides when they thought that the engine had 'put paid to you'."

This was the beginning of my friendship with Mannock. He was twenty-eight or twenty-nine and had then been two months in France. Everything about him demonstrated his vitality, a strong, manly, yet human vitality. His alert brain was quick to elucidate a principle, and an unbroken courage and straightforward character forced him to take action where others would sit down uncomprehending. I was awed by his personality.

Mannock walked with McScotch, showed him to the hut he would live in and introduced him to his room-mate, Lieutenant Lionel Blaxland. Seeing his new comrade settled in, Mannock left him to the unpacking of his kit and the writing of his first letter home from the front. McScotch was surprised later, when at dinner, Mannock sat silently, not speaking a word to him. McScotch retired to his hut depressed and feeling very lonely. Ten minutes later, it was an even different Mannock who appeared at his door. McScotch describes this occasion:

"Well, young fella," he said, adopting a 'Pukka Sahib' accent, "Like to take a constitutional with me?" and then, in his natural voice, "Want a walk Mac?" There was a clear-cut, incisive timbre in his speech, not exactly Irish but with the definite enunciation and pure vowel-sounds of the Celt.

Thoroughly delighted at being 'noticed' again by this 'seasoned' pilot, I put on my belt and cap. Mannock had changed into slacks, and his pale yellow socks and tie showed that regulations regarding dress were slightly relaxed at the front. His forage cap, soft round the edge, was poised on his head in the recognized Beatty angle. His carriage was more alert and springy than it had been when wearing his heavy flying-boots, but there was something ungainly in his walk, as if his ankles or knees were stiff. Why it was that on the first evening I should feel an overwhelming sympathy for him because of his walk I do not know. A man's step can reveal such a great deal of his character and emotions, but Mannock's method of walking puzzled me, filled me with a sense of pathos.

He was silent as we came out onto the road and turned towards Bruay. His face was set with an almost painful expression, and I glanced at him covertly several times, waiting for him to speak.

Knowing him so well afterwards, I can surmise what was going on in his mind as we passed the hangars. His thoughts probably were: "This is a new fellow. His first impressions are going to be indelible. Wonder what type he is? Seems fairly decent, but I'll soon find out. Anyway, he's new and inexperienced. I'll give him the chance I've never had."

His first question towards 'finding out' was typical of the way he attacked everything. "Are you a snob?" he fired at me, giving my face that same penetrating scrutiny as when asking about the 'spin'. "Snob? How do you mean?" I asked. "If you are thinking of social snobs, then I'm not. We each have our own particular forms of snobbery—about intellect, character, ability, honesty and, I suppose, courage." "Well answered!" he exclaimed. "But snobbery is a nasty word. I only apply it to social and money snobbery—the empty social type particularly. There are so many damned social snobs about."

He then proceeded to fire question after question at me, about my home, my education and my religious beliefs. This inquisitiveness might have aroused some antagonism in me had it not been accompanied by a directness and understanding that one rarely discovers so quickly in strangers. He wanted to estimate my character and my spirit, not my social position.

Sitting by the roadside, Mannock told McScotch of his past and then invited him to have a drink at the local *estaminet*. There, Mannock explained, they would see "the youngest, prettiest, sweetest and most innocent thing you have ever met". Over a glass of *champagnes aux cognac* McScotch was introduced to Odette and was then ignored as Mannock beamed lovingly at the girl, a blonde only sixteen years of age. Darkness fell, and the two new made friends walked back to camp, only the thunder of the guns at Ypres booming out to remind the happy men that they were at war. Twenty years later, McScotch would write:

I thought it strange that Mannock was disliked to varying extents by the others in the unit, while everyone he met outside the Squadron liked him immensely, civilians and

other Squadrons' pilots alike. After knowing him for some
weeks, the answer to this became obvious. To cover his
'nerves' during his first days with 40 Squadron, he had
jumped in to any conversation and talked continuously to
hide his fears and worries. This, and his initial lack of success
and apparent lack of effort in the air, brought about a situation where Mannock was shunned by many in the Squadron.
He amplified this by withdrawing from their company and
concentrating on his work. After settling down to the job in
hand, he became more like himself and made friends,
although these were mostly outside Squadron circles. These
friendships helped him immensely. He desperately needed
companionship and found it invaluable for his peace of mind.
Had it not been for the support he gained from his relation-
ships, I seriously doubt if he would have been able to keep
himself together mentally and have developed his skills in
the air.

Mannock was indeed developing in the air. Although his
luck had not changed, he was now becoming more aggressive and threw himself at German aircraft whenever the
opportunity arose. Seeing his potential, Major Tilney
allowed him to lead patrols, and by his actions Tilney
appears to have been the only man to recognize Mannock's
need for encouragement. The confidence and experience
that was to result from such help would soon pay divi-
dends. With every trip over the lines, Mannock was
getting closer to the enemy machines—but his first two
close encounters with the Germans were not reported.
    On 25th May he led 'C' Flight onto two German observa-
tion-machines. One of the Huns was too high to be
attacked effectively, and after 'putting the wind up him',
Mannock turned on the other. He saw the strangely coloured machine float into his sight and opened fire. His
heart sang as the well tended Lewis hammered out thirty
rounds and riddled the area around the enemy pilot's seat.
The German flyer put his nose down slightly and carried
on. Mannock was convinced of the kill but failed to report
it on his return. None of his colleagues had seen the fight,

and he feared their response to any claim he might make for an unconfirmed victory. He had to hold back his disappointment as he walked away from his aircraft after landing. At least he knew of the success—that was reward and encouragement enough.

A week later he had another encounter which provided even more encouraging results: "*2nd June 1917*. . . . Led the patrol yesterday (five machines) and had a scrap. Emptied a full drum of rounds into a big, coloured two-seater Hun from about 25 yards. Must have riddled the bus, but nothing untoward happened. She put her nose down and went straight."

Although both of the Germans Mannock attacked had shown all the classic signs of a wounded or dead pilot, he once again refused to report his fight. He would wait, he thought, until he had a definite kill, one which would be in no way suspect and provide ammunition for his critics. The numbers of these critics had decreased considerably as he became more aggressive, and during the following days their numbers would fall to almost zero. No one in the unit could deny the improvement in Mannock. He felt happy in the new friendly atmosphere of the mess and revelled in his nickname of 'Mick'.

Confidence mounting, Mannock had two more engagements on 1st and 5th June—a balloon near La Bassée which failed to ignite and a two-seater which went straight down in a steep dive. He mentioned nothing of these combats to his comrades and sat alone in his hut that evening, praying for the first opportunity to hand in a report of victory.

To the mechanics standing on Bruay field on 7th June, there was nothing special about the way Lieutenant Mannock glided in for a landing. They had come to ignore his rather bumpty, wing-straining landings. When he leaped from his cockpit, however, his shouting and whooping could be heard over the entire field, informing everyone that something was indeed different about "mad old Mick". Bounding across the grass, he stormed into the

Recording Officer's hut and breathlessly told his story. He could not contain his flooding emotions as Major Tilney signed the combat report, the proof that his kill was officially accepted. Walking over to his hut, the still cheering pilot read his copy of the report.

COMBATS IN THE AIR

Squadron	:	Forty	Date :	7 June '17
Type and No. :		Nieuport Scout	Time :	7.10 am
Of Aeroplane		B1552		
			Locality:	North of Lille
Armament	:	One Lewis Gun		
Pilot	:	2/Lt E	Duty :	Escort
		Mannock, RE		
		RFC		
			Height :	13,000 feet
			Result :	One EA out of control

The cold language did little to abate Mannock's joy. Nothing, he knew, could erase his happiness in success or the memory of that wonderful fight.

Mannock had been part of an escort to a formation of FE2b bombers which had set out to bomb the town of Lille. Within seconds of their arrival over the target, a flight of Albatros scouts had come down on the slow-flying FEs and were themselves attacked by the protecting Nieuports of 40 Squadron. Singling out a German who was pulling in behind one of the bombers, Mannock rushed in with all possible haste. At 10 yards from the Albatros he opened fire, sixty rounds from the Lewis gun being sufficient to kill the pilot and tear his machine to pieces. He was surprised when he felt sorry for the dead German as he fell away in his shattered aeroplane.

Mannock could have claimed this machine as being destroyed rather than out of control as he was certain of its destruction and the death of the German flyer. However, regulations regarding kills were strict, and he would have had to have found a witness. But whatever the report called his victory was irrelevant. He was happy beyond description in the knowledge that he had triumphed over the enemy and, more importantly, over his fear.

Yet another unconfirmed kill followed on 9th June, an Albatros scout falling before his gun, but once again he was unable to confirm the kill.

Six days later, he was beginning to feel frustrated at his inability to obtain confirmation. Two Huns had been hit by his fire and headed for the ground as if crippled, but Germans and British alike were known to feign death as a means of escape. Mannock resolved to bring a kill down behind the British lines. That, he felt, would bolster his reputation and let him see the results of his shooting at first hand. His frustration was to grow, however, as the Germans refused to fight, usually fleeing when Mannock and his companions appeared. Then his second flying-accident, on 12th June, almost put an end to his developing spirit of aggression.

Mannock was flying over the field at 120 mph after a patrol over the line. Lining the Nieuport up for landing, his vision was suddenly obscured by a blinding flash of pain. His eyes streaming with tears and his brain hammering with intense pain, he somehow brought the scout in to land safely. He was pulled from the cockpit and carried to the Medical Officers' quarters where attempts at first aid caused him to faint. Taken to hospital, cocaine was injected, and under its effects the surgeon extracted a piece of grit from his heavily inflamed right eye. Further visits produced yet another foreign body which turned out to be a piece of steel from the Nieuport's cowling.

Excused operational duty during this time, Mannock spent his time flying over to visit neighbouring units and talking over his new frustration—not being able to fight when things were only just starting to go right for him.[3] The break from fighting also had another, more worrying effect on him. Unable only to concentrate on his fighting-

---

[3] According to legend, Mannock's left eye was useless, but as his right eye was covered after this accident and he was still able to fly, it would appear that the left eye was in good condition. See closing chapter.

technique, he began to notice the strain which his nerves had suffered during the weeks of almost constant battle. In his diary he recorded: "*14th June, 1917*. Feeling nervy and ill during this last week. Afraid I am breaking up. Captain Keen very decent. Let me off some flying for today. I think I'll take a book and wander into the woods this afternoon although rather threatens rain. Oh! For a fortnight in the country at home!"

Three days later, the exhausted Mannock was fully recovered from his eye-injury and sent home on leave. The following two weeks at home would be a mixture of happiness and sorrow.

4
Flight Command

Walking down the street to his mother's home, now in Birmingham, Edward Mannock looked forward to the rest and relaxation that was sure to come during his leave. Quiet nights with his family, home cooking, excursions into the city—all these, he knew, would set him up for his second tour at the front. But as Julia Mannock opened the door to her son, he realized that his dreams of home were about to be shattered drastically.

Kissing him on both cheeks, the haggard woman took him by the hand into her sitting-room and poured a large measure of whisky, a measure which he could see was not her first of the day. Staggering across the room, Mrs Mannock asked after his health in a drawling mumble. After a number of interruptions, Edward gave up his attempts at making her understand what was happening in France and changed the subject by asking of life at home. At this she began an angry and violent speech concerning her family. Although Paddy Mannock had continually sent her money, times were hard, she said. No one came to visit her. Jessie was having troubles with her marriage and had become a "loose woman—a hussie". Edward, she demanded, should send her money; could he not remember what she had done for them all as children? "It's your Christian duty, Eddie, your duty."

Mannock left his mother's house as soon as possible. Each day in her company had been hell. Her drinking was getting worse by the hour, and although he was sorry for the old woman, he could no longer see her as she had been. Boarding the Wellingborough train, he knew that he could

no longer be part of that unhappy, broken family. The
Eyles would see him through on his leave; they were his
family now.

Mannock's return to the Eyles' home was a much
celebrated event and one which Jim Eyles remembered
well:

It was good to see him in his uniform and looking fit and well.
He bounded into the house, and it seemed as if he didn't stand
still from the moment he arrived until the moment he left. He
spent hours telling of the events which he had been unable to
mention in his letters. The censor would have cut out any
mention of his actions and flying. After making sure that we
were all right and assuring us both that he was 'in the pink',
he spent most of his remaining time with us discussing air
fighting and talking of the new methods he was evolving. I
couldn't say how many hours I spent in these talks with him.
He would get me to simulate a German plane with one of my
hands and tell me to move around the room in a certain
fashion. Standing on chairs and tables, he would use his hand
in a like manner and demonstrate how he would tackle Huns
in various situations. He became completely lost in these
experiments; everything had to be worked out in detail and
be realistic. He used a lamp to represent the sun, I remember.
Once or twice he became angry with me when I forgot what he
had told me about how the Hun (myself) would react to
various forms of attack. I had never seen him so involved in a
subject, and that is saying a great deal in Pat's case. He left us
in fine spirits, sure of his coming success.

Mannock rejoined his unit on 2nd July and immediately
went to see McScotch in hospital where he had gone after a
minor accident. The 'new' Mannock was evident to
McScotch as soon as his friend strolled into the ward and
sat by his bed. He had obviously done some thinking while
on leave. He spoke of the power within each human being,
a power which, if directed properly, could overturn the
largest of obstacles. After a great deal of thought, he told
McScotch, he had come up with some ideas about fighting
and was going 'all out' from the first second he crossed the

German lines. Mannock would have to wait ten days,
however, for the Germans to overcome the timidity they
had been showing since the end of 'Bloody April'.

On 12th July Mannock climbed into his new Nieuport
Scout, B1628, and headed for the lines. He was looking for
trouble and soon found it south-east of Lens. Spotting two
DFW two-seaters, he turned away from the Germans and
climbed to 11,000 feet over Avion. Manoeuvring above and
behind the enemy, he darted in suddenly on the rearmost
aircraft and loosed off a burst of ninety rounds. The large
German machine slipped into a turning dive and headed
for the ground obviously out of control. From a height of
7,000 feet, the jubilant Mannock watched the craft turn on
its back and crash upside down behind the British lines at
Avion. Immediately on landing at Bruay, he boarded a
tender and set out to salvage the wreck. What he saw on
arrival at the crash site would stay in his memory for the
rest of his life.

The remains of the DFW lay crumpled in a heap in the
centre of a muddy field, its skeleton stripped bare by
souvenir-hunters. The observer, a captain, had survived
the crash and was by that time in hospital; the NCO pilot
lay beside his machine under a gas-cape. Mannock lifted
the cape and forced himself to look upon the gory sight.
The body had been horribly mutilated in the crash, and the
effects of the fire from the Lewis gun could clearly be seen
around the dead man's head. After his inspection of the
fallen foe, Mannock moved to the aircraft. His diary records his feelings at the time:

. . . the little black terrier—dead—in the observer's seat. I felt
exactly like a murderer. The journey to the trenches was
rather nauseating—dead men's legs sticking through the
sides with puttees and boots still on—bits of bones and skulls
with the hair peeling off, and tons of equipment and clothing
lying about. This sort of thing, together with the strong
graveyard stench and the dead and mangled body of the pilot
combined to upset me for a few days.

Mannock gained much knowledge from his trip to the trenches, most of all the certain knowledge that he would surely have gone insane had he been drafted to the Army and been forced to live in this man-made hell of mud. To McScotch, however, his revulsion at what he had seen was not immediately evident. He later wrote of Mannock's return from the crash-site:

> With great emotion Mick described the mangled condition of the pilot's body—blood and bones. Horrified and disgusted with him, I remarked reproachfully: "I'd never like to see the smashed-up body of a man I'd killed." He looked at me queerly for a few seconds, then his eyes softened.
>
> "Neither would I, old boy. It sickened me, but I had to see where my shots had gone. Do you know, there were three neat little bullet holes right here," pointing to the side of his head.
>
> He then explained to me that he had fired his gun so often without hitting the enemy machines that he had begun to think that he could not see a target correctly. "No matter how much nausea it caused, I had to find out, and this one down on our side was my only chance. I've missed so many of them, and I wanted to know for sure," he added almost plaintively.

On the following day, 13th July, Mannock was attacking the Germans with even greater energy. A two-seater went down out of control near Douai, as did another only one hour later.

To his critics in the mess, Mannock had 'come out of the woods'. Many apologies were made, many friendly comments passed. Up until the last minute, two of the critics, Godfrey and Hall, were passing a barrage of comments concerning Mannock's courage. In the end a rift was developing between various factions, and the senior officers became worried. Attempting to salvage the decreasing morale of the Squadron, Major Tilney detailed Captain 'Zulu' Lloyd to question Mannock on the subject. For Lloyd, this was a difficult task, as he had been impressed with Mannock from their first meeting and had become quite friendly with him. Relaxing in the easy-going company of the big South African, Mannock immediately surprised Lloyd by admitting outright that he had been terrified when facing the enemy and that he had held back in combat. In his forthright manner, he continued:

"Of course, I've been frightened against my will—nervous reaction. I've now conquered this physical defect and, having conquered myself, I will now conquer the Hun. Air fighting is a science. I have been studying it and have not been unduly worried at not getting Huns at the expense of being reckless. I want to master the tactics first."

Lloyd was satisfied with the man's straightforward answer. He had thought of having him sent back to his regiment as unfit for flying duties, but any such thoughts were dispelled during their short talk. When told by Lloyd of his talk with Mannock, most of the major critics accepted what had been said. Some refused to believe Mannock's story, and even his victories of the 12th and 13th could not change their minds. Mannock put this down to jealousy and from then on ignored the men in question. A new sense of unity was evident in the mess.

This fresh spirit was to last only a few days, however. Disaster was only days away.

Flying the late patrol on 21st July, Bond, McScotch and Kennedy were horrified by the sight of a burning aircraft in the sky over the German lines. Bond headed for the scene hoping to engage what might be left of an enemy patrol but, due to their petrol running low, had to return to Bruay. On landing they were informed that the flaming torch in the sky had been their dear friend Lieutenant Rook.

Rook had been one of the most popular men in the unit, and his death affected them all severely. Only nineteen, he had shown character and wisdom beyond his years and was developing into a first-class pilot. His death was to have a greater effect on the unit over the following days. After months of continuous fighting the nerves of every pilot were strained to the limit of human endurance. Daily they risked a horrible death over the lines—falling helplessly out of control and waiting for the impact to bring death, or the death most dreaded by all pilots: flames.

The death of young Rook initiated a wave of speculation as to what could be waiting for them in a matter of hours or even minutes. A number of pilots put their now obsolete machines to blame. Others went as far as to blame the mess piano which had been used by all the Squadron's casualties. It was, they said, cursed, and soon no one would go near it. McScotch, his temper rising, put it down to a more practical and tangible reason: The Germans had long been accused of using illegal incendiary ammunition to ensure the destruction of a machine although only a few rounds might strike it. McScotch had decided to follow their example. The death of Bond on the 22nd finally convinced him to continue with his plan.

After seeing the much loved Bond blown out of the sky by 'Archie' fire, McScotch, his hands trembling with emotion, headed home with a great hatred in his heart. Later he ordered his mechanics to wheel out his Nieuport and prepare her for flight. As the plane was fuelled, he asked one of the mechanics, Davidge, to fill the ammunition-drums with a special mixture of bullets. McScotch describes the occasion:

When they hit us, we are 'finished', but two or three mornings previously I had emptied a drum of our own clean ammunition into a two-seater without any apparent effect. I decided to remedy this by a concoction of my own by filling my drums with the three types of ammunition, 'Armour-piercer', 'tracer' and 'Buckingham incendiary' (normally only used against balloons). Such a mixture would certainly prevent the next enemy escaping.

The first indication of the level to which my 'morality' had fallen was provided by Davidge. He was a very clever mechanic, much older than myself; his greyish hair always gave me the idea that our positions should have been reversed as far as rank was concerned. He did not refuse to fill my drums as I wanted. He drove it home to me much more effectively.

"I'll do it if you order me to, Sir, but if you are caught with such ammunition on you, it will mean death for you on the other side and court martial for me here."

Determined to have my mixture, and prepared to accept full responsibility, I carried the three drums over to the armoury hut and locked myself inside. It took me ten minutes to fill the first drum, for I had to lay the cartridges out in order and test each for a sunken or defective 'cap'. This was a frequent cause of stoppages, and as it very often jammed the gun beyond remedy in the air, we had to take every precaution. Cursing the Germans, the Kaiser and the profiteering manufacturers who made it necessary for us to examine ammunition that had been 'passed' in the munitions factories, I was surprised to hear a timid knock at the door. I asked who it might be, and Mannock's voice replied: "Let me in, I want to speak to you." On my opening the door for him, he came inside, shut the door slowly after him and stood leaning against the post. Conscious that I was doing something 'dirty', I could feel the tension in the air as I waited for him to speak first.

"What are you doing there?" he asked, knowing very well, because he added, "Your mechanics have just told me."

"Mixing some filth and corruption for the Huns," I said angrily. "I'm going to make sure of the next one I hit."

Filling the remainder of the drum mechanically, one tracer, one armour-piercer, one Buckingham, I glanced at him several times without meeting his eyes. Something had upset him. His face was haggard, and he was nervously pulling the strap of his Sam Browne. When I was about to commence filling the third drum, he put his hand on my arm. He was trembling. "Look here, Mac, if you have any affection for me, forget about last night and this morning and let me empty out that stuff." I stopped and sat down on the bench, facing him.

"It isn't only poor old Rook. They've never fired anything at me but incendiary, and two mornings ago I missed a two-seater. If I had had my drums loaded with this, I've have got him—properly." He stood silently looking at me—almost tearfully and, in support of my own wavering brutality, I continued: "I'm out to do as much damage as I can, and the surest way, no matter what it means, is the best for me.

Besides, it isn't like you to care about how they die as long as we kill them."

Again his challenging eyes met mine: "Do you mean to say, Mac, that you would coolly fire that muck into a fellow creature or worse still, into his petrol-tank, knowing what it must mean?"

I realized then that the hardening effects of the war had been greater on me than on Mick; or that he was attempting to play on my emotions.

"Well, if I can't do anything with you, I may as well go and leave you to it, but I'll give you one last chance. If you won't chuck it for humanity, will you for me?"

He had come down to our old footing. "If you'll tell me exactly why you are so upset about," I replied. His eyes filled with tears.

"Because that's the way they're going to get me in the end—flames and finish. I'm never going to have it said that my own right hand ever used the same dirty weapons. The other fellows all laugh at me for carrying a revolver. They think I'm doing a bit of play-acting and going to shoot down a machine with it, but they're wrong. The reason I bought it was to finish myself as soon as I see the first signs of flames."

And so started another phase in the relationship of Mannock and McScotch. Mannock had bared his soul completely and from that day on would confide totally in his friend.

While Mannock took off later that day, a telegram was speeding its way towards Bruay field. McScotch read it: "2nd Lieutenant Mannock awarded the Military Cross."

McScotch ran to his quarters to change and then to Mannock's hut to collect the crumpled old jacket which only Mannock regarded as smart in appearance. Throwing the uniform into the back of the Squadron car, McScotch headed off towards the town of Béthune at full speed.

Mannock returned later in the day from a particularly cold and numbing flight. Sitting on the edge of his cot, he stripped off his layers of oil-stained clothing and then stopped as he noticed something odd about his coathanger. His spare tunic jacket was hanging there, and Mannock rose to examine it. He had left it in a suitcase, he was sure, but now it had been moved by someone. Turning the garment around to inspect it, he noticed a length of purple and white ribbon above the left breast pocket. McScotch had made good use of his time in Béthune. He had purchased a length of the ribbon which represents the Military Cross and persuaded a woman to sew it in place before rushing back to Bruay.

Mannock was delighted with the award but, with customary modesty, allowed the event only one line in his diary, a line which comes nowhere near to describing his emotions at the time: "I heard officially yesterday that I have been awarded the MC."

The official citation was more enthusiastic: "In the course of many combats, he has driven off a large number of enemy machines and has forced down three balloons, showing a very fine offensive spirit and great fearlessness attacking the enemy at close range and low altitudes under heavy fire from the ground."[4] There were also fine words to accompany the medals and the personal congratulations of General Trenchard (OC the RFC in the field); the opinions in the mess were, however, somewhat less complimentary, for Mannock's old reputation was taking a long time to die. He was called "soft", a "pandering type who licked the CO's boots", a "madman who would soon lose his head with success".

The critics were given yet more reason for complaint when Mannock was promoted to temporary Captain in command of 'A' Flight. Most of the men had come to accept him as a lone fighter and could see little hope for him as a leader. Even McScotch wondered if the success would be too much for the already strained mental stability of 'Mick'. When the early morning patrol on 23rd July left Bruay for the front, Mannock, over-excited by his official rewards, proved his critics to be right.

[4] This citation was written later, when Mannock had achieved more successes which the citation includes.

He led the patrol at full speed towards Valenciennes and, seeing no signs of enemy activity, turned back towards Douai and Henin Leitard, usually good hunting-grounds for the British fighters. According to McScotch:

Mick was on the *qui vive*, looking out for low-flying enemies, but there was nothing on which he could lead the flight. Excitement at the promotion, combined with the knowledge that four or five other pilots were bound to follow wherever he led, may have induced a feeling of power and a greater determination to meet the enemy. Mick's behaviour, however, annoyed me: it bore out several of the things that had been said about him. I had hoped that he would take things quietly until the flight got used to him.

Filled with disgust at seeing in my friend what I thought was another manifestation of the wrong side of the war mentality, I determined to leave the patrol as soon as opportunity offered.

At 12,000 feet, Mannock led his men below a large cloud-formation where they would have been easy pickings for the German fighters. McScotch had a reasonable excuse for leaving the flight and climbed above the dangerous clouds. After a short fight with two German observation-machines, the rebellious pilot flew home, by this time having forgotten his actions against Mannock.

As McScotch filled out a report concerning his contact with the enemy, he became aware that he was being watched. Looking up, he saw the face of Mannock by the door. Before he could finish and speak to his friend, Mannock had turned away to walk across the aerodrome, his helmet dangling against his leg, his head bowed.

That evening, as McScotch sat in his hut writing, he noticed the lone figure of Mannock walking to and fro past the tennis court, obviously trying to attract the attention of his friend. Seeing this, McScotch made for the door and called out to the dejected-looking figure.

"Want your constitutional, Mick?"

"Yes, alright, if you want to come—with your Flight Commander."

The two men laughed, and then Mannock continued: "Yes, I don't think a serious talk will do either of us any harm." They walked towards Bruay village, neither man talking until half way towards the village when Mannock turned to his companion. "You hurt me like hell this morning, Mac! Why did you leave the flight?" McScotch considered lying to save the man's feelings, but Mannock's directness deserved an honest answer: "Because I meant to hurt you." Mannock walked on slowly, still listening to McScotch. "You know how much I admire your courage and your brain, and how glad I am to see you getting a reward for all your work. But seeing the change in you since then, I was worried that the charming fellow who looked after me so well when I first arrived had only the ordinary standard of values after all. The fact that you have achieved some success means nothing to me. I have always admired you as a man, in favour or disrepute, for what you are in your mind." Pointing to Mannock's medal ribbon, he continued, "Don't tell me that that makes any difference to what you think of yourself." Looking closely at McScotch's eyes, Mannock thought over what the man had said and then spoke. "Hell, none at all. Come on old man, you win every time. I suppose it's because you've been to university. I'm going to study."

Settling happily into their renewed friendship, the two men headed into the village for a meeting with Odette. This form of relaxation, McScotch knew, would complete the resealing of their comradeship. The following days in the air would show a change in Mannock the leader.

An examination of his combat record at this time shows his more careful attitude. His previous 'quick rate of kills' diminished rapidly as he made it his main business to look after the patrol and learn the skills of leadership. He did manage to shoot down at least two EAs during the three weeks leading up to 5th August, but the slower pace of combat demanded by his responsibility made him moody.

An opportunity to fight, on 12th August, did much to renew his enthusiasm. Alerted by a telephone call from the front line, he raced to his waiting machine and took off in pursuit of a German balloon-raider. Once in the air, he flew south-east and arrived just in time to spot an Albatros making its first attack on the British balloon line. At the sight of Mannock's machine, the enemy airman turned away and ran for home. Using every ounce of his skill, Mannock soon came within striking distance of the black-painted Albatros, although the superior enemy craft was capable of greater speed. Short bursts of fire from his gun forced the German to weave and thereby lose ground; Mannock slowly closed the range. Seeing the Albatros flying straight and level for a few seconds, he darted in and sent off a burst of twenty rounds which sent his opponent down, out of control. The German airman maintained sufficient control during his 1,000-foot descent to hold the machine level for a soft crash landing.

Mannock was thrilled with his victory; his smile returned at the thought of the fight. The pilot, Leutenant Joachim von Bertrab, had been wounded in both arms and a leg, and Mannock was pleased that the German had survived. His pride shows through clearly in his diary comments: "Two machine-guns with a thousand rounds of ammunition against my single Lewis and three hundred rounds. I went up to the trenches to salve the bus later and had a great ovation from everyone. Even Generals congratulated me. He didn't hit me once." The wings of von Bertrab's machine were inscribed with Mannock's name and hung as a Squadron trophy in the hangars. American reporters interviewed a blushing Mannock and turned his clipped answers into much-romanticized sentences.

Recognition meant little to Mannock though. The knowledge that he was succeeding at the business of air fighting was reward enough. He found it hard to believe that, only four months before, he had considered himself a wanton coward who should be expelled from the service. He was a success as a fighter, but the matter of his skill as a leader was still in the balance. The lesson he had learned from McScotch's rebellion had been forgotten to an extent; a more extreme lesson would be needed before he would realize his mistaken idea of leadership.

At a dinner to celebrate Mannock's success against von Bertrab, a plan was evolved to shoot up Dorignies aerodrome and the German Squadron then in residence, Richthofen's 'Circus'.

Substituting Kennedy for McScotch, who had mechanical troubles with his Nieuport, Mannock led the flight off the ground at 6 am on 13th August. No sooner had the trio crossed the lines than they were met by a formation of Albatros Scouts and, although outnumbered by three to one, Mannock waded into the German formation, determined to 'show 'em'. After their first, unsuccessful pass at the enemy, the Nieuports found out to their horror that the German pilots were of a stouter breed than they had encountered before. Fighting desperately, the British only just succeeded in holding off the strong attacks on each of them, at the first sign of a break in the onslaught, Mannock led his men out of the fray.

Back at their home base, the full extent of the German attacks could be seen. Tudhope, the second pilot of the formation, had been cut to pieces. An explosive bullet had burned through his main wing-spar; his top wing was cut to ribbons by bullets; his instruments were smashed, and a bullet had passed through his collar. Mannock and Kennedy fared somewhat better, although their machines would be out of commission for days. McScotch ran over to Mannock's plane and arrived in time to greet him as he climbed down slowly from his riddled cockpit.

"Get any of them, Mick?"

"No," replied Mannock pulling off his oil-stained helmet, "My only concern was to save my blooming skin. Thank God we're back anyway."

Later, in a nearby hotel, Mannock revealed to his friend the full extent of the day's fighting on his attitude. "For the first time I realized that my friends' lives were in my hands. It might seem obvious to you, but it has only just hit me that I can't go on fighting like a loner when I'm leading the others. I don't want to lose any of you."

Mannock's sincerity was well displayed over the following weeks. In combat, his attacks became more calculated; on the ground he spent most of his time improving the flight's tactics and formulating new methods. The men of 'A' Flight noticed the daily changes in his leadership as he tried out his various ideas in the air. Gone were the headlong rushes at the enemy; now he would stalk them and place his men in a favourable position, the finesse of these tactics improving daily. Once the opposing formations had joined in battle, it was every man for himself, twisting and turning to gain a killing-position on the tail of an enemy, firing quickly and pulling away sharply to avoid the shots of any opponent trailing behind.

Kills still came Mannock's way during this period. On 15th August he sent one Albatros scout down and had two other combats which, although he was certain of the planes' destruction, could not be claimed as he was engaged with other enemies and could not observe the crashes.

'A' Flight became the most successful and happy band in the Squadron. Old differences were forgotten as Mannock developed his own skills and used them to the benefit of his followers. Confidence in their leader grew with each trip over the lines, and this new trust in him led to increased efficiency.

On 16th August, Mannock sent down three EAs and a DFW two-seater, and two more DFWs on the following morning. Seeing the enthusiastic waves of his men on the return flights from such combats, he began to feel more wanted and necessary than he ever had in his life. Not only was he playing a part in the war by destroying Germans, he was protecting other men and assisting their efforts against the enemy. Leadership and team tactics were the answer, he decided; gone forever were the 'lone wolfs' of the war's early days. In this way was sown the seed from which would blossom 'Mick' Mannock's eventual greatness.

Mannock, McScotch, Tudhope and Kennedy became inseparable companions during the fighting of August. In the air or on the ground they were rarely apart for long: flying together and relaxing together after a fight. To Mannock, the war was now becoming one gigantic game. Gone were the days of gloom and despondency; he had his work and his men—what more could a man ask for? The death of Kennedy on 22nd August was the first reminder that war was not a game.

On that evening Mannock took a patrol of ten Nieuports to shoot up five German airfields. After leaving two of the selected targets smoking, the flight encountered seven enemy scouts near Douai. Mannock's keen eyesight spotted the Germans early on and allowed him to climb 'up sun' of their group. Giving his signal for the attack, he heeled his machine over and pounced on an unsuspecting Albatros. Twenty-five yards from the target, he raked the German craft from nose to tail and watched it go down completely out of control.

Turning to fight, Mannock saw two of his men going down steeply and being followed by two Germans who were pouring fire into the hastily departing British. Racing to the scene, he fired wildly and succeeded in throwing the Germans off their track. The first Nieuport pulled out gently, but the rearmost continued in an ever-increasing dive. A large white number '4' on the doomed machine was illuminated in the dying rays of the sun—Kennedy. Mannock almost forgot about the fight in his horror. The first of their happy band was gone.

The hand of death had once more come close to Mannock, and the effect on him was severe. The thought of death, and the various ways in which he might meet his, became foremost in his mind. His calculated style of fighting had removed any ideas of dying he might have had previously, but now he had a cold reminder of his own mortality.

After landing, Mannock did his best to console the grieving members of his flight in an attempt to stop the death of Kennedy from affecting their morale. That night, however, McScotch was to see how the death of their much-loved comrade had affected Mannock himself. McScotch heard the sound of a man crying loudly as he approached Mick's hut. On entering he saw yet another side of his friend. Mannock sat on the edge of his cot, his head clamped between his knees, his body rocking back and forwards. His face was covered in tears and saliva, and from his mouth could be heard the muttered words: "Ken, oh Ken, why you, why did you have to die?" Over and over again, Mannock repeated the words, 'keening' for the dead in the old Irish way. He failed to notice McScotch's presence.

Kills still came his way, but none would give the thrill that he had previously experienced from victory.

Within a period of three hours on 4th September, he sent down three enemy machines: two DFWs and an Albatros scout. (One of the DFW two-seaters had horrified him as he had been close enough to see the bloodied face of the observer hanging out of the fuselage.) Sensing that he might make his score up to four for the day, he began to feel a partial renewal of his old pre-battle excitement and took off alone in search of number four.

Holding the Nieuport at 10,000 feet over Avion, Mannock scanned the skies and soon spotted an aircraft in the distance. He strained to focus on the approaching machine but failed to identify its nationality. Quickly, he decided on a move to establish the craft's identity. He turned and flew in the same direction as his quarry, knowing that, if it was a British machine, it would ignore him; if a German, it would probably attack. Flying straight and level at a lower altitude than the fast-moving machine, Mannock waited excitedly for the possibility of attack and looked over his shoulder. He had almost given up hope of the machine being German when his ruse proved fruitful. As it dropped into a dive towards his tail, Mannock clearly saw the black Maltese crosses on its wings. He prepared his machine for a fight and settled his nerves as he waited for the German to come closer. As the enemy pilot settled into a flat, attacking glide, Mannock hauled the Nieuport around and down and then climbed swiftly above and behind the now confused German. Looking through his sight, he concentrated on the large two-seater and ignored the fire of its gunner in the rear cockpit. The pilot of the two-seater weaved and side-slipped to give Mannock a difficult target, dodging in and out of the Nieuport's sights. Firing controlled bursts of four and five rounds as the German came into his field of fire, the tense British flyer pressed his attack. Seeing his danger, the enemy attempted to turn away but was too slow to avoid the killing burst from the steeply banking scout.

Mannock continued firing as he saw pieces of metal and wood fly off the enemy's fuselage and large holes appear in its fabric. As the last bullets slammed into the doomed machine, he pulled away and watched the plunging German. His joy at the sight, however, was instantly turned to horror. A small gleam appeared through the gashes in the German's forward fuselage, hardly noticeable at first but then growing bigger in size and intensity. Mannock had seen aircraft burning before, but this was different; he had set it alight with his own hand. The flames grew rapidly until only a fireball remained in the sky. Mannock would not have been able to recognize the object as having been a machine which had contained two human beings, apart from the one or two identifiable objects which broke away from the flaming mass and floated to the ground as separate small blazes.

He sat high in the sky and watched the disappearing wreckage as it fell out of his view, so taken up with the terrible sight he had just witnessed that he would have been completely unaware of the entire German air force if at that moment it had been flying alongside him. His head fell to his heaving chest, his stomach churning violently. Through closed eyes, he could still clearly see the disintegrating ball of fire and the flailing arms of its occupants, smell the acrid stench of its trailing ribbon of smoke.

On his flight home, Mannock thought continually of the burning German airmen. The fight grew to enormous proportions in his mind, the image of the burning mass expanding into an indelible picture he would never forget. For some reason which he could not understand or explain, he knew that this victory was different in some way. It had not been a particularly difficult fight, but something about it was different. The flames, he thought to himself, might have something to do with it, but why should he feel so bad about killing men in one way rather than another? Mannock was unable to find an answer; he knew only that the burning DFW would stay in his mind forever. A chill wave of fear ran down his body at the thought of his victims and their charred remains on the muddy fields of Petit Vimy.

Over the following three weeks, Mannock continued his experiments with 'A' Flight, the emphasis mainly on team tactics and formation attacks. When not in the air, he could be seen sitting by himself, a large pile of notepaper in one hand while his other hand scribbled furiously at some diagram or calculation. The members of his flight left him to his work and waited impatiently for him to call them to his side for yet another of his 'Plannings'. He would suddenly rise from his seat, clear a table in the mess and excitedly call their attention to his latest idea. Whether it had been the effect of the burning German which brought about his lack of interest in the development of his personal score, no one knew, but to each man in the flight, it was obvious that 'Mick' had changed and that something was growing in his mind. After outlining his latest ideas to the men, Mannock would make for some quiet spot to continue his thinking.

In the air he became less dashing and reckless. He took greater care when leading the flight into an attacking position and would stay with them during a fight as much as possible. His rate of success slowed down considerably over this period, only four Germans falling to his gun in twenty-one days. Three of these victories grew dim in his memory within days; he even forgot to claim one of them in his combat report. One, however, had a more lasting effect on his memory.

On 20th September, over Hulloch, Mannock attacked a DFW two-seater and sent it crashing in flames. Although slightly less horrified by the sight of his second 'flamer', he could not stop his mind from confronting him with the image of the first DFW he had burned. The memory of that previous kill took over in his mind to such an extent that the descent of his second burning German went almost unnoticed. He once again thought of that kill of 4th September. It began to assume a strange importance in his mind, became an Albatros around his neck.

His growing fear of the DFW's memory was abated little by the award of a bar to his Military Cross on 14th October. The arrival of his rest period two days later was received with little enthusiasm.

An examination of Mannock's letters and recorded conversations at this time provides an important insight into his mental state at the time of his second leave period, in October 1917. He was approaching that emotional crossroads in his service which is noticeable in the careers of most of the leading pilots of the Great War. With the possible exception of James McCudden VC, most pilots passed through this most dangerous of phases in their development. McCudden considered air fighting to be a series of mechanical acts designed to destroy the enemy machines, and he gave little thought to the men he was killing. To less calculating pilots however, the effects of months of fighting on their emotional stability was unavoidable.

After seven months of almost continuous fighting, Mannock was approaching this sometimes lethal period. Although sickened by the daily butchery he witnessed around him, he became resigned to staying at the front and began to look forward without enthusiasm to the leave which most pilots prayed for. The threat of death or total nervous breakdown became unimportant, as did the hope of a spell at home. Had Mannock not become increasingly devoted to the development of his flight as an efficient fighting team, it is most probable that he would have become reckless and foolhardy in his fighting as did so many other men at this stage in their service.

Returning from leave, he arrived back at the front to join in the Battle of Cambrai. Aircraft were used extensively in this attack to support the ground troops and tanks—a dangerous and nerve-tearing business of flying over the enemy trenches to bomb and machine-gun the German columns. When he was carrying out this daily duty during November, Mannock's nerves suffered greatly, and his score against the enemy airforce was not increased. In December, the Squadron was re-equipped with an aircraft which Mannock hoped would put an end to their losses against the superior German machines. However, his first trials of the machine were to prove frustrating.

A product of the Royal Aircraft Establishment, the SE5a fighter had arrived at the front amidst great speculation about its potential prowess. It was rumoured to be vastly superior to anything being used by the enemy, and great hopes were formed on the basis of its reputation. Mannock was thoroughly impressed when he first saw the new machine. In contrast with the small, frail Nieuports, the SE seemed every inch a fighting aeroplane. Equipped with a 200-hp motor, it was capable of 120 mph and climbing to a height of over 19,000 feet. Its square-rigged lines were unattractive compared to the more streamlined designs then in service, but the new fighter had been designed for strength rather than appearance.

After being informed that he was to fly SE5a number B665, Mannock walked out to his allotted machine and climbed into the cockpit. He was instantly impressed with the SE. It was obviously a strong and well-thought-out design. His long frame settled easily into the roomy pilot's position which afforded great protection from the biting

cold of high-altitude flying. Checking over the instruments with his keen eye for detail, Mannock then spent
much time examining the features of his mount which
attracted him most, the two machine-guns with which the
aircraft was fitted. Apart from the single Lewis gun
mounted on the upper wing, as it had been on his old
Nieuport, he was highly pleased by the sight of a heavy
Vickers gun which protruded back into the cockpit. Sighting along the gun, he looked forward to the damage such a
weapon would inflict on the Germans. No more would the
British be forced out of a fight to change the ninety-round
drums of their Nieuport Lewis guns. The Vickers would
fire five hundred rounds before stopping—more than
enough, thought Mannock, wiping the gun—five hundred
rounds backed up by 270 in three drums for the Lewis. He
climbed down and walked around the rugged brown craft.
Running his hand lovingly along its surfaces, he looked
forward to the next patrol over the lines.

After seeing the attention Mannock paid to his new
machine and hearing the praise he had given to its qualities, it was with some surprise that the mechanics and
riggers of 40 Squadron listened to his comments after
returning from his first patrol in the SE. Mannock landed
heavily on the snow-covered ground of Bruay and jumped
from the cockpit as soon as the machine rolled to a halt.
From the glaring expression on his face, it was obvious to
everyone that the commander of 'A' Flight was in a mean
mood. He walked quickly over the frozen ground, stripping
off his flying-clothes as he went. Muttering under his
breath, the angry pilot headed for his hut and loudly
slammed the door.

Over the next few days, several faults appeared in the
SE. The Hispano engines had an annoying tendency to cut
out without warning, and the guns were giving much
trouble to the disappointed pilots of 40 Squadron.

Mannock's own dissatisfaction with the new aeroplane
was further increased by an almost lethal incident over
the lines. While making for Bruay after a test flight over

the German lines, he was horrified to hear his engine misfire and then come to a halt. Unable to re-start the dead motor, he was forced to put the SE into a shallow dive in order to maintain speed—an action which brought him closer to the German-held ground. By skilful flying, he only just managed to make the British front-line trenches and 'pancaked' the machine gently down on the mud. As this was on Christmas Eve, the trenches were quiet, and Mannock had to wait for three hours before being rescued. During this time he was constantly sick, due to the sight of hundreds of corpses which littered the area. Stranded without "even a smoke", he was severely depressed by the sight of so many unburied corpses, some of which had been lying uncovered for months. Rats picked constantly at the decomposing flesh of these grisly grey cadavers and ignored the stooping figure of Mannock as he vomited against the side of the machine.

The numerous reports regarding the fighters' weak points soon reached the ears of General Trenchard at RFC Headquarters, and he decided to visit the complaining units in person. While Mannock was over the lines on his seventh patrol with the troublesome SE, he was unaware that Trenchard was awaiting his arrival with interest.

Trenchard's eye was drawn to Mannock's machine as it landed along with the others of 'A' Flight. He watched the heavy landing and the careless fashion in which the SE was taxied into the flight line. Turning to a nervous Major Tilney, he asked for the name of the pilot. "It's Mannock, sir," said Tilney trying to remain calm. Tilney well knew Trenchard's reputation and feared his meeting with an equally fiery Mannock. Not noticing the presence of his superiors, Mannock sprang from the SE and proceeded to list its faults once more for the mechanics' attention:

"Look at this damn gun—the Vickers—look at it. Useless! Only fired two blasted rounds and then stopped dead. Jammed! If I'd had my old Nieuport, I could have bagged two nice juicy huns."

Trenchard's ADC stepped forward to take command of

the situation and asked Mannock for his overall opinion of the machine.

"The machine's OK, but not with these engines and guns—useless. Give me back my Nieuport."

Tilney suggested that they all retire to the mess where they might discuss the subject more fully. As Trenchard turned to walk across the crisp snow, Tilney took advantage of the break in conversation to pull Mannock briefly to one side.

"Mick, be more tactful, will you? He is the commander of the RFC after all, you know."

"Sorry, Major, but if it gets me back my Nieuport and gets rid of these hulks, then I don't care what he thinks."

McScotch had by this time walked over from his craft and attempted to abate Mannock's temper. He reasoned that Mannock was at no greater disadvantage when the Vickers failed; he still had the Lewis gun and was therefore as well armed as he would have been on the Nieuport.

"Yes," admitted Mannock, "but what's the use of carrying an extra gun that's no damn use to you? It fires slowly, and if the thing's wrongly adjusted, it blasts your prop' to bits. The general staff should do something about it, but they won't if we don't do some shouting."

Major Tilney blushed as Mannock's comments reached the ears of General Trenchard and felt furious with the angry pilot for causing an unnecessary fuss in front of the General. Two days later, Tilney would apologize to Mannock when the result of his outburst became known.

Grounded by a spell of especially severe weather, Mannock sat with his pilots in the mess and waited for a break in the snow. A silence fell over the company at the entrance of a stranger. Unable to see the man's rank under his wet trenchcoat, Mannock rose to greet the newcomer. "Good afternoon, stranger. Take off your coat and come into the warm. Orderly! A drink for our guest." Removing his coat, the stranger noticed a change in Mannock's expression as red staff-officer tabs were revealed—he always reacted to 'tabs' with much hatred. The stranger's next statement was all that was required to burn the remnants of Mannock's short fuse.

"I'm the Gunnery Officer at headquarters. I've come over to have a . . ."

"You mean you have something to do with those blasted guns of ours. Orderly! Quick!"

"Yes, Sir?"

"Get me a hatchet," ordered Mannock.

"A—hatchet, sir?"

"Yes, a hatchet, now hurry it up. I want a hatchet."

But suddenly Mannock's expression of hatred disappeared, and he approached the now terrified Gunnery Officer. "Perhaps now you will know exactly what we feel about those guns. What will you have to drink?"

Sitting by the fire, the Gunnery Officer explained that Trenchard had been impressed with Mannock's forthright comments on the SE5a and had ordered an immediate investigation. He had also ordered that each pilot be instructed in the use of 'CC' gear which synchronized the Vickers' gun's fire to the engine speed and allowed bullets to pass through the propeller arc without damage. The investigation proved Mannock right about the shortcomings of the SE and more especially the equipment fitted to it. The guns were not only wrongly adjusted, they had been lubricated with a grease which was unsuitable for the French winters and froze as soon as the SE climbed to operational height. The Hispano motors were also found to be faulty in manufacture, having been part of a rush order to meet the need for more powerful motors at the front. These faults were corrected in a short time, although they were to cost the lives of many airmen before satisfactory solutions were found.

Test flights with the improved SE convinced Mannock of its worth. He became fond of the machine and saw in it the perfect vehicle for developing his plans of attack on the enemy. It was during a lone test flight that he first triumphed over an enemy while using the SE.

On the morning of 1st January 1918 Mannock had
taken off alone for a trip over the lines. He felt pleased
with the SE as it purred smoothly through the air towards
the front. He revelled in its stable flight-characteristics
and positive response to his control-movements. Opening
the throttle wide, he pulled back gently on the stick and
sent the roaring SE up into the sky until he reached 15,000
feet. Over Fampoux he eased back the throttle and sat
back as he scanned the ground below. As the cockpit clock
showed 11.35 am, he spotted a swiftly moving speck
against the sun's glare. Identifying the speck as a German,
Mannock gunned his engine to full power and climbed
further into the cold sky.

A thousand feet below, in the German Hanover, Leutenant Wilhelm Klein had no idea of Mannock's presence.
Both he and his observer made continual sweeps of the air
as the British lines were close and the threat of attack was
great. The sound of the rear-gun firing caused Klein to
look round. A British fighter was screaming down to
attack, its speed making it an almost impossible target for
his frantically firing gunner. Klein increased his speed
and turned to meet the SE. At precisely the right moment,
Mannock eased back his throttle and levelled out behind
and below the German machine. A slight pressure back on
the stick sent the SE rocketing up towards his prey, the
momentum gathered in his dive being used to maximum
effect. Pressing both gun-trips, he sent off a burst of a
hundred rounds and immediately saw the effects of the
withering fusillade. At first the Hanover shed a number of
small parts of its structure, and then Mannock saw larger
objects sailing past him as the German craft began to
crumple in mid-air. As the stream of bullets churned up
the upper wings' centre section, the craft fell to pieces, its
wings floating gently to earth as the heavy fuselage dropped in a steep dive to the ground. With unbelievable force,
the Hanover crew were slammed into the ground, and
their machine was reduced to powder. Mannock rolled the
SE over and dived for his own lines.

That night, he enjoyed a farewell dinner given to honour
McScotch and himself as both of them had been ordered
home on leave. Mannock felt well pleased in the company
of the men who had come to mean so much to him, though
only a few of the men present were 'Old Hands', most of the
original Squadron members with whom he had first served
having been killed or transferred. It was hard for him to
believe that he, after starting in the Squadron as an extremely unpopular newcomer, was being fêted in this
fashion. He looked around at the smiling faces of his
companions.

Major Tilney and McScotch were the closest friends he
had made amongst the original members of the unit. His
heart gladdened at the thought of how they had survived
the previous nine months of terrible war. Two men at the
end of the table caused his heart to warm even more, as
they sat together talking of their chances at the front. Both
were good men, Mannock felt, one perhaps better than his
companion and destined for great deeds.

The man in question was Lieutenant George McElroy.
He had arrived in 40 Squadron looking much like any
other new arrival, but Mannock had taken an instant
liking to the young Irishman, and they soon became close
friends. Another pilot present at this dinner, William
Douglas, writes:

> He and Mick were great antagonists and friends. Mick
> fathered McElroy in his inexperienced fighting days. In spite
> of their heated and seemingly bitter arguments on Irish
> affairs, they would always disagree agreeably. It is a good
> thing Mick was able to sport McElroy's potential within
> hours of their meeting. McElroy, or 'McIrish', as Mick named
> him, was very headstrong and would probably have been
> killed early on had it not been for Mick's tuition and patience.
> He was the first of Mick's pupils in the true sense. He took an
> interest in the lad from the first and coached him daily. Not
> only did this teacher-pupil relationship prove fruitful for
> McElroy and enable him to become one of our top fighters, it
> also taught Mick a great deal about other men.

This relationship had indeed had a profound effect on Mannock. He had seen the results of encouragement given to inexperienced pilots in the past, but it was with McElroy that he discovered himself as a mentor and learned the basic skills which were to enable him to become the greatest of all teachers in the air force.

He discovered that not only the teaching of fighting skills could make a raw pilot into a great fighter—that was only part of the necessary exercise. Mental attitude of the right kind was absolutely essential if the men were to do a first-class job against the enemy. He felt sure that he had the answer to the problems then prevalent amongst pilots arriving at the front for the first time: skill and team-work in the air, comradeship at all times. Mannock looked forward to his next posting where he could put these ideas into action. If only someone had helped him in such a way when first he arrived in France. In the midst of success and the adulation of his men, Mannock had to suppress a tear as the memory of those terrible first months at the front came flooding back. The accusing stares of his fellow pilots, the comments which were widespread behind his back, the terror he had felt when going over into enemy territory. His train of thought was broken not by the noise which was by then rolling around the mess room but by the sudden memory of the 'flamer'. The image of its burning bulk shot into his mind even though it had not been connected with any of his previous thoughts. The burning DFW had become a ghost which haunted him almost incessantly. Nothing could stop its memory from plaguing his thoughts. With great self-control, Mannock forced his hands to stop shaking and rose amid tremendous applause to make his parting speech. William Douglas writes:

He had been sitting quietly for some minutes, deep in thought. We often saw him like that, far away, it seemed, looking at some distant object that only he could see. He rose and entertained us to one of his marvellous speeches. I can't exactly recall the contents or subject, but it was probably on his favourite subjects for such occasions: beating the hell out of the Hun and making friendly jokes about various members of the mess. These sessions would have appeared rather brutal at times to outsiders, non-RFC types that is. He would include jokes about one or other of his comrades going down in flames or crashing in some other horrible way. There were times though when one could sense that he was not being humorous about these 'flamers' and did in fact believe that they were going to take place. At the farewell dinner to Tudhope some months later, he foretold the fates of himself and McElroy. Within the fortnight both were down. That was the last time I ever saw him. He was idolized by all who came into intimate contact with him, and for me he was the outstanding personality of the war.

Major Tilney wrote in the Squadron diary that night: "His leadership and general ability will never be forgotten by those who had the good fortune to serve under him."

For Mannock and McScotch, though, their hectic service with '40' could not be allowed to end in so peaceful a fashion. At 11 am on the morning of 2nd January, Mannock's packing was interrupted by an excited McScotch. Between them they had agreed to fly just one more mission over the lines, although it was considered to be tempting the fates to fly with a leave-pass in one's pocket. With three hours to go until the leave-tender arrived to pick them up, they might just be able to find one more German to add to their list.

Mannock sprang into his machine and was quickly into the air. Major Tilney had been alerted to their unauthorized mission by the sound of Mannock's engine and appeared in time to question McScotch.

"Look here, Mac, you can't go up. You're already struck off the strength of the Squadron."

"Hang it all, Major," replied McScotch still climbing into his cockpit, "Mick's gone up, and I'm supposed to meet him over the lines."

Seeing that any protest was useless, Tilney waved

McScotch away with a smile. "OK, Mac, but I don't know anything about it, right."

Mannock and McScotch returned two hours later without having had any success. Climbing down from the B665 for the last time, Mannock bemoaned the lack of any Germans in the sky and muttered as he walked away, "They wouldn't even come out to say good-bye."

But his sadness at missing a lost chance at the enemy was dispelled by the sight of an old friend in the mess, James McCudden. Since their first meeting at Joyce Green, when Mannock had been a pupil, the two men had become close friends, meeting whenever their individual duties allowed. McCudden was also on his way home for a well deserved rest and joined Mannock and McScotch on the journey in the company of McElroy and another new pilot, Wolff. Staying overnight in Boulogne, Mannock awoke the next morning and joined his companions for breakfast. He was met by much laughter in the dining-room as the happy pilots gave vent to their high spirits. As Mannock watched his friends demolishing large plates of bacon and eggs, his expression changed and gave them yet another target for their excited humour.

"Have some food Mick, the grub's great."

Mannock grimaced and replied, "Please don't even mention the word, will you. The Channel is as rough as blazes, and I must confess I'm the world's worst sailor."

McScotch laid down his knife and fork. "Well I'm blowed. After seeing you throw an aeroplane about the sky, I can't see how you can possibly be seasick."

Mannock took a small bite from a thinly buttered slice of toast and, through a weak smile, said, "That cross-Channel steamer hasn't got a joystick you can waggle."

Landing in Folkestone the following day, the friends had little time to talk before going their respective ways. Mannock clasped McScotch firmly by the hand. "Well, have a good time old man. We'll be back for the big fight and then—sizzle, sizzle, wonk!" They made arrangements to meet during their leaves and parted, never to meet again. McScotch was posted to a training-programme in England as it was considered that he would be more use there. His record of twenty kills with 40 Squadron had little effect on the officials who decided such matters, and he would never return to the front.

Mannock would experience similar difficulties with the 'red-tape Brigade'. Before the first day of his leave had passed, he had decided to return to active service long before his thirty days' leave and the following two months of home service were completed.

5
'The Iron Man'

Three months after his last meeting with McScotch, Mannock was still on home service. The leave period had proved uncomfortable for him, his mother's drunken states being particularly unbearable. His relationship with the Eyleses had also proved incapable of making him settle down to enjoy the resting effects of his time away from the war. Jim Eyles remembered the change in Mannock:

He was like a cat on hot bricks from the moment he arrived until he left. He was convinced that the early part of 1918 would see a great German advance on the ground accompanied by heavy fighting in the air. Whatever the cost to his health, he was determined to get back to the front in time to take part. At first I thought his nervous state might be due to the rather unpleasant time he had experienced at home with his mother and family, but it wasn't. His mother had been very drunk, he told me, and his sister had become what he called a 'loose woman' after the breakdown of her marriage. He spent most of his time doing the rounds of the various departments in the War Office. As each of these offices gave him the same reply, that he was invaluable as an instructor, he returned each day to sulk and bombard us with a storm of impolite comments concerning the officials and 'staff types' he had met. His only relaxation, if one could call a man in his state relaxed, was usually found at the RFC Club in Bruton Street, London. On one visit to the club he took me along, and I was pleased to see him come to life amongst his old comrades. But even these visits tended to depress him. All the talk of fighting and old friends from the front, reminded him even more of his 'desk job', as he referred to it.

Mannock was posted to Biggin Hill aerodrome where he flew FE2s on radio-testing flights. Boredom and frustration set in as he spent each day flying around the field receiving and transmitting radio signals. One weekend, he could stand the job no longer and headed for London with Eyles to "blow off a bit". In the RFC Club he met General Henderson, and a most tense collision took place. Jim Eyles was at Mannock's side during the meeting.

The General asked Mannock how long he had been home. Mannock replied, "A month too long, sir." Henderson then told him that he would have to remain at home for perhaps another two months or more. This statement finished off Pat's last reserves of politeness. "If I can't get back to France soon with permission, I shall get back without permission. I shall take a machine out of the hangar one day and fly back to my old Squadron."

To this Henderson replied, "If you do that, Mannock, you'll be court-martialled and shot."

Mannock replied, "Death is better than dishonour, sir!"

I felt relieved when Henderson relaxed his stare at Pat and smiled at him admiringly. "You win, Mannock. I'll see what can be done."

After this he cheered up somewhat although got rather angry when refused permission to take an SE up at night to hunt for German bombers over London. I don't think he could stop fighting at all.

Two days later he received some news which went part of the way towards relieving his boredom. He wrote to Eyles:

Just got my instructions. As you know, I have been trying very hard to get out to France again. Well, I have been posted to No. 74 Training Squadron at London Colney, and we are proceeding overseas next month. Hooray! I feel horribly glad about it. We shall be flying the same machines as I flew in No. 40 Squadron—SE5s.

Later that same day Mannock received another letter which was not so pleasant. Opening the envelope he found a note which read: "The enclosed was dropped by a German scout and picked up by the infantry. Records show that it refers to one of your victories." Mannock opened the small, stained envelope and read through the smudged contents: "The 4th September I lost my friend Fritz Frech. He fell between Vimy and Lieven. His respectable and unlucky parents beg you to give any news of his fate. Is he dead? At what place found he his last rest? Please to throw several letters that we may find one. Thank. . . ."

Mannock crumpled the letter into a tight ball and let his forehead fall to his desk. 4th September—the DFW—the 'flamer'. Before, it had been a horrifying vision in his memory, a falling aeroplane which he had set alight: now 'it' had a name; 'it' had parents and friends. Perhaps as much for his own sanity as for that of the dead Frech's family, Mannock wrote a kind note explaining that Leutenant Frech had died bravely in combat and had been killed instantly.

The flamer had returned to haunt him—the first in a new series of hauntings.

Mannock arrived at London Colney on 1st February 1918 and was immediately taken in by the trainee pilots of 74 Training Squadron. At first he had been worried about being an instructor rather than going straight back to the front, but the welcome he received abated any regrets about his posting. Many of the trainees had already seen action as observers and had little time for the aloof non-combatant instructors they had previously served under. But Mannock was obviously different. In him they found a leader who could give them the benefit of his experience and to whom they could relate.

Bad weather and bad instructors had had their effect on the unit's morale, and the new flight commader set about correcting this situation with great energy. The tall, scruffy figure of Mannock would be seen darting about the aerodrome. He went from building to building, searching out any signs of despondency. On entering a room where the atmosphere was not 'right', he would go into a display of almost lunatic comedy to raise flagging spirits. Bursting in on a scene of gloom, he would run from one man to the next shouting: "All tickets, please. Pass right down the car. Let the old man see the Hun." To the new pilots, this action on the part of an instructor was completely unbelievable. Previous teachers had not even consented to entering the trainees' mess, never mind joking with their trainee 'Huns'. Mannock watched the stunned, silent faces about him and then launched into his next attempt. "Right—who's for a beer?" A stuttering pilot rushed up to the bar and shouted, "Quick, waiter—beer." Mannock patted the lad on the shoulder and smiled his broad smile. "I want no waiter, but I could do with a beer."

Within twenty-four hours of his arrival, Mannock went through this routine many times, each time proving a success. In this short period, he had succeeded where many had failed. He made personal contact with his men from the start, setting up a rapport with each and every one of them.

The results of his efforts were noticed easily at the lectures he gave on air fighting. These had never been attended fully in the past, and those who had made the effort to attend were usually to be seen yawning with disinterest. Mannock's lectures, however, were different affairs.

His friendly relations with each of the men, combined with his personal experience of aerial warfare and successful record, made him an instant success in the lecture-room as much as it contributed to his success in the mess. He set about tearing down all the barriers of regulations and 'form' which he believed were useless in the training of an efficient squadron. As long as each member of the unit pulled his share of the workload, Mannock forgot about the non-regulation clothes and lack of parade-ground etiquette. The success of his methods was closely monitored by the Squadron's Commanding Officer, Major Alan Dore. Any worries by Dore were soon relieved by the sight of each trainee throwing himself into the course of

instruction and thronging around the unconventional instructor, seemingly desperate for some small snippet of
information.

Mannock's lectures became the highlight of each long
working-day, and he revelled in the enthusiasm of his
pupils. Facing his first class, he waited for the men to settle
down and then opened his lecture: "Gentlemen, always
above; seldom on the same level; never underneath." This
was his motto for successful air fighting, and he continually hammered it home to his men. The words were
painted in large letters on the sides of hangars and walls,
never allowing anyone to forget the dictum.

His lectures were illustrated verbally by his memories
of particular combats, explained in practical terms. Each
pilot would be asked to suggest a tactic which he felt would
counter the move of an enemy in battle; Mannock set the
problem, the pupil answered, and Mannock would then
explain any faults in the reasoning of the novice. With
patient care and attention to the needs of each of his men,
he built up a feeling of great confidence among the young
pilots. One of his pupils later said: "Mannock convinced us
that with a little practice we could knock the hell out of the
best Hun. He was not a total success as an instructor. He
admitted that it was as much as he could do to fly himself.
He was almost as bad at landing as I was, and there were
many occasions when I had the pleasure of pulling him
from the wreckage of his 'bus'."[1]

On 7th March the trainees waited for the results of their
efforts to be posted along with the final selection of pilots
who would go to France with the Squadron. Thirty-two
pupils and seven instructors were competing for the
twenty places; tensions ran high as to the results.

The three flight commanders were to be: Mannock 'A'
Flight, Captain Young 'B' Flight, Captain Cairns 'C'
Flight. Many of the pupils were severely disappointed at

[1] Contrary to this popular opinion about Mannock's ability in the air,
many of his contemporaries regarded him as a "good" or "excellent"
pilot.

not being selected, but six of them were especially pleased, for they had been chosen to serve under 'Mick' Mannock in 'A' Flight—"Lieutenants Roxburgh-Smith, Dolan, Howe, Clements and Atkinson—'A' Flight. Captain Mannock MC."

Seeing the smiling throngs of men round the notice-board, Mannock formed an idea of how to help them celebrate the event. Walking quietly up behind them, he spoke in a strange voice, his accent obviously intended as a parody of the brigade's chaplain: 'O pilots of the illustrious 74th hearken unto me. I want you to fall in outside in the mess." As soon as the men had 'fallen in,' Mannock addressed them once more: "You shall follow my movements." At this he set off on a trip around the base, his voice booming to the strains of 'Keep the Home Fires Burning' and 'Rule Britannia'. Stopping for a moment every 50 yards or so, he would perform a series of exaggerated exercise movements, knee-bends and toe-touching. Refusing to alter course to avoid the buildings occupied by the more senior members of the Squadron Staff, Mannock continued through their offices, over desks and chairs and whatever else he found in his path. The Squadron Adjutant, a Guards officer named Everard, was not at all amused. Luckily for Mannock, other senior officers were well pleased to see such high spirits amongst men soon to leave for the front.

After a two-week course at the Air Fighting School at Ayr in Scotland, the Squadron returned to find a new commanding officer. Major Dore had been serving continuously at the front for two years and had been granted a much-needed rest. In his place the men of 74 found a most striking figure, Major Keith Caldwell MC, a New Zealander who had built up a reputation as a determined fighter during his time with 60 Squadron. There he had fought alongside such famous fighters as 'Billy' Bishop, Chidlaw-Roberts and Meintjes. Like Mannock, he was striking in personality and appearance, tall, well built, with black hair and a chin which could not deny his strong character. The great 'Jack' Scott, whose opinion of air fighters was respected throughout the Flying Corps, estimated that Caldwell (or 'Grid', as he was known) had engaged in "more fights for the number of times he had been in the air than any other pilot".

Caldwell's first talk to his men indicated that he was cast in the same mould as 'Mick'. Announcing that he had been given command of 74, 'Grid' told them:

You are being equipped with the finest fighting aircraft in the world and are particularly fortunate in having three experienced flight commanders. I'm sure we will be a very happy family. When we get to the war, you must all fight like hell. It must never be said, however, that a pilot of 74 ever failed to go to the aid of a comrade, even if he is in a position to knock down a dozen Huns. Any man failing to assist another in trouble will get the pleasure of my boot up the backside. I need not point out, gentlemen, that I have big feet.

Major Caldwell remembers Mannock at this time:

I had met him once before when he was in 40 Squadron and had been impressed with his dedicated keenness to get as many Huns as possible. I was happy to see him as flight commander when I took over 74.

He was a tall, thin man, about 6 feet, with reddish-brown hair and a ruddy complexion. He spoke rather quickly and sounded nervous in a way. He didn't sound Irish as has been mentioned in various books. Not exactly Public School, but a pleasant warm mid-English. He was a striking figure to see, always carried a cane! I had every confidence that Mannock was just the right type to inject the right sort of attitude into the chaps and give them a good chance when we got up against the Hun.

Thus the scene was set for 74 Squadron's future: teamwork, aggression in the air, and comradeship at all times. Caldwell's speech had a lasting effect on everyone present; no pilot of 74 Squadron ever let his comrades down during the time they were in France. The combination of Caldwell and Mannock was unbeatable. They set about tearing down the myths and superstitions that were rife in the RFC at that time. Regulations were enforced only when necessary, and morale was given great importance.

One of Mannock's pilots at this time was Lieutenant Harris G. Clements. 'Clem' writes of his first meeting with Mannock:

I first met Mick in March 1918 at London Colney where 74 were training. I had been out on a training-flight with 'Taffy' Jones, and Mick must have spotted my neat three-point landing. I was never a 'great pilot', but as good landings were quite something in those days, he must have been impressed. He asked which pilot had been flying the SE with blue wheels and later asked me if I wanted to go to France with the Squadron!"

Mr Clements also remembers Mannock's efforts at building up the unit's morale:

When he first joined 74, he would organize sing-songs in the mess. Singing at the top of his voice, he would play on a collection of cans, tankards, pots and pans, and glasses, tied to the back of a chair. He also had a proper drum which he played loudly. Soon we would all join in and get a 'jam-session' going.

We developed into a family really, Grid and Mick saw to that, an efficient, happy team. They both threatened to shoot down the first man who left a chum in trouble with the Huns. On the rare occasions that gloom did settle on the mess, Mick was just the man to handle it. He didn't give a hoot how he did it, as long as the men ended up happy and morale was maintained. He was always the life and soul of the party, although this never interfered with our respect for his authority.

On the same point, Major Caldwell writes:

He was very easy-going on the ground and liked everyone to be free and happy. In the air he expected a high standard of flight discipline, such as close formation-keeping and not wasting ammunition. He was quick to ask for any of his men who did not toe the line to be transferred, and there were times when he had to be reasoned with as sometimes his earlier assessments were a bit hasty. It had to do with his rather excitable nature, I think.

On 25th March 1918 the Squadron was ordered to be in France by 1st April, and the men were given a last leave-pass before departure. Mannock asked Clements to spend part of his leave with him at the Eyleses in Welling-borough, a clear indication of the regard he had for Clements. After his last visit home, Mannock had only the Eyleses to go to for privacy and refuge. He valued his visits there highly, and only Clements was ever invited to this sanctuary of Mannock's. Clements recalls:

We flew up to Wellingborough and landed in a field where we were picked up by car. We visited Jim Eyles and his wife and later had dinner at the Hind Hotel in the town. I was surprised by the number of people Mick knew. It seemed as if the whole of Wellingborough had turned out to greet him. Some of the guests were local 'bigwigs' whom he got on well with.

On 30th March the Squadron left for France and by 11th April were settled into their new home at Clairmarais near St Omer. They were now listed as No. 74 Squadron, Royal Air Force, the Royal Flying Corps having been absorbed into the Royal Navy Air Service and renamed the RAF. On arrival at Clairmarais, the news that each pilot was waiting for was announced: 74 would make its first trip over the enemy lines on the following day. A coin was tossed to see which flight would make the first patrol, and Mannock was furious at losing his chance of 'getting over' on the dawn patrol.

At 6 am the following morning, Mannock was on the field to see off 'C' Flight on their first patrol. He walked from machine to machine asking each pilot not to disturb the Germans in case they were not around for his patrol later in the day. 'C' Flight returned later to announce that they had had no success, but they had run into a very aggressive German patrol and had been in a most difficult fight.

At 8.25 the same morning, 'A' Flight took off to find the first victims of No. 74. Climbing to 15,000 feet over Merville, Mannock spotted a formation of Albatros Scouts and led his flight down to the attack. Leading the diving machines into the centre of this large formation, he lined up a German in his sights and sent it down to crash to the east of Merville. Dodging between the swirling mass of aircraft, he kept an eye on his men and was pleased to see Dolan send a second Albatros down out of control. 'A' Flight had been bloodied in battle, and Mannock had scored the first kill on the record of 74. Approaching Clairmarais, he led his flight down low over the field for a celebratory 'beat up'. Firing signal-flares of all different colours, the pilots demonstrated their extremely high spirits. One pilot was not so happy, however. Clements had suffered badly during the patrol and was criticized by Mannock:

On my return to the aerodrome, he was waiting for me. "You won't do for me, boy," he said. I was in no mood for polite conversation, having had a dreadful time on the patrol. I had lost the formation, got 'archied', lost the Lewis drum in a dive and was extremely sick due to flying on an empty stomach. I rounded on him. "Look," I replied, "I lost you, and if you think I'm yellow, fill your tank, and we will go over together, as far as Berlin if you like." After this I never had any trouble and flew as Mannock's wing man. One could say I became his shadow.

Mannock proceeded to liven things up for his victorious flight during the remainder of the afternoon. He wanted to ensure that no one would have too much time to reflect on the more unpleasant events of their first fight. He knew well that the sight of their two victims going down to crash might stimulate the imaginations of certain pilots, and the morale of the unit might be affected in turn. At 2 pm he led them off the ground for the second patrol.

Near the Bois de Phalempin, Mannock signalled the presence of the enemy to each of his men and then swooped down to the attack. Two minutes later a black-and-yellow Albatros was falling in pieces. Joining up with Mannock for the return flight, the men of 'A' Flight waved their congratulations to their leader on his second success of the day. On arriving home, they were surprised to learn of his report concerning the flight. Looking at the formally worded report-sheet, they read with surprise: ". . . The whole flight should share in the credit for this EA, as they all contributed to its destruction."

Major Caldwell remembers:

I would judge that Mick let at least four or five claims go in favour of others in his flight. It may be difficult for someone who wasn't there to appreciate the effect this could have on an unblooded pilot. To have even one German machine on his record instilled a great deal of confidence. He would not hand these out piecemeal; he had to feel that the pilot was worth the encouragement. The main thing about Mannock was that his successes were won in front of his followers; they could see how it was done. His tuition and example were of great value to the flight and the Squadron as a whole.

Following each clash with the enemy, Mannock would call his pilots together for a discussion about the handling of the fight. During these talks, the pilots became aware that he could see much more in the air than they thought possible. He could relate what had happened to each of them during a combat although many aircraft had been involved in dozens of separate fights. After discussing each pilot's actions against the enemy, Mannock would continue with his favourite method of training. Lieutenant Giles, who was to gain much from these lectures, recalls the form they took:

Although Mick had been compared with von Richthofen in a number of books since the war, he was the exact opposite. Mick was more in the mould of Voss and fought each combat as he found it; von Richthofen used planned manoeuvres for a fight. Mick made us imagine a situation and then asked for a quick answer. In this way we started to 'think' and 'eat' air fighting. You could be relaxing on the field, talking about home or whatever, when he would appear suddenly and throw questions at you. Practice in the air and his training-sessions made us react automatically and instinctively to any situation which arose in a fight.

One of Mannock's 'star pupils' at this time was Lieutenant Dolan. In a letter home he wrote:

Mick (Mannock) goes down on his prey like a hawk. The Huns don't know what's hit them until it's too late to do anything but go down in bits. He goes down vertically at a frightening speed and pulls out at the last moment. He opens fire when only yards away and then 'zooms' up over the Hun and turns back for another crack at the target if necessary.

I saw him attack a two-seater that way and could see how confused the Hun pilot was. He didn't know where Mick was or where he would appear next. After opening fire, he half rolled over the top of the Hun and dived down underneath him. While the Hun was trying to locate him, Mick appeared behind and below and tore the EA to shreds.

It was Lieutenant Dolan who first saw the more blood-thirsty side of Mannock's training-methods:

It was 30th April and Mick took me up to 'see me right' as he put it. I was in need of encouragement at this time, but I had no idea of how he planned to give me it. Looking back, it must seem a little blood-thirsty, but it worked. Near Poperinghe, we spotted a Hun two-seater, but Mick just kept flying on as if it didn't exist. I knew how good his eyesight was and waited for the signal which I knew must come shortly. But instead of signalling for me to go down with him, he told me to stay where I was. All the signals are given by hand-movements and moving the aircraft in various ways. By this time we were circling around the Hun and had the sun behind us. When we were almost directly ahead of the EA, down goes Mick like a rocket. He positioned himself so that the pilot could not see him because of the upper wing, and the observer was looking the other way for the expected form of attack from the rear. He gave it a quick burst and then pulled up a long, curving climb to join me. As he pulled alongside, he waved his arm down at the running German and nodded at me to get it. I went down on the Hun's tail and saw that Mick had killed the gunner, and I could attack safely.

He had set the Hun up for me and deliberately killed the gunner to ensure that I got my kill.

Mannock was now in his element. The flight was developing into a first-class unit, and its reputation was spreading amongst the neighbouring Squadrons. The men of 74 felt supremely confident under his leadership. Their natural fears were suppressed to an absolute minimum, thereby allowing for an extremely high standard of concentration on the job in hand. The effect on the pilots of his dynamic personality was great and, in at least one case, survives the intervening sixty-one years. Mr Clements writes:

I will feel proud to have been a member of 74 Squadron and have always regarded Major Caldwell as a very brave man. Naturally Mick Mannock was my hero. Flying with him was such a wonderful experience, he was such a clever leader, and our patrols were like hunting-expeditions. I have always considered myself very fortunate that he chose me to serve in his flight, and it is still my belief that this is the reason I am alive today. It might sound strange, but I was never afraid to cross the lines or engage the Huns when Mick was there. It seemed impossible to get caught when he was running the show. Mick had a much more organized approach to air fighting than did other patrol leaders. Most leaders tried to look out for enemy machines on their own, but not Mick. We were each expected to scan a particular section of the sky while he kept an eye on the air below us. If we spotted anything, we

would fly alongside him and waggle our wings. We would
point out what we had seen, and Mick would decide on the
action to be taken. We would inform him of any changes in
the enemy's position, and in this way he always had an
up-to-the-minute picture of the situation. We were never
surprised by the Hun, which can't be said for many outfits.

The high spirits of 74 were tested to the limit on 21st
April. 'B' Flight had become involved in a fight with four-
teen German Scouts near Armentières which soon developed into a swirling mass of machines, each trying to
avoid collision with another. From the midst of the twisting horde fell a blazing aircraft, and a quick count by the
British leader, Cairns, told him that the falling plane was
British. Lieutenant Begbie had become the first member
of 74 to die in combat, and the horrible way in which he
died would have a profound effect on each member of the
unit.

On announcing the news of Begbie's death back at their
base, the shocked young pilots were surprised to see Mannock and Caldwell walking around the men present and
ordering the organization of a party. That night in the
mess after dinner, the pilots of 74 were shocked to see
Caldwell and Mannock playing games of 'mess rugby' and
pulling each of them in turn into the sprawling mass of
men as they rolled around the room. Certain of those
present could not understand the behaviour of their comrades. How, they asked Major Caldwell, could he play
games when one of their friends had only that afternoon
gone down in a burning SE? Caldwell called for a halt to
the game and lined his men up for an explanation: "The
death of anyone amongst us must never be allowed to
affect our morale. We will have a 'full out' guest-night
whenever anyone is killed; that's an order."

Mannock stepped forward into the centre of the assembly and raised a glass to toast the death of Manfred von
Richthofen, who had also been killed that day. "Gentlemen, raise your glasses to Lieutenant Begbie and also to

Baron von Richthofen," Mannock paused, "in the hope that the bastard also went in flames." Mannock smashed his glass to the ground and then turned to Lieutenant 'Swazi' Howe, who was the smallest man in the Squadron. Taking the small South African by the shoulder, he smiled. "Now my fine young fella, it appears that we have lost our ball during this brief break in play. I take pleasure in announcing that you are now 'it'." Picking up the protesting Howe, Mannock threw him to the waiting crowd and then jumped on top of the men himself to send them all crashing to the floor.

And so it was when death came to one of their company. The heavy fighting of April and May 1918 would give cause for two more such 'celebrations', for Bright, Skeddon and Stuart-Smith on 8th May, and for Dolan on 12th May.

The loss of Dolan had a profound effect on everyone, especially Mannock. He had become friendly with Dolan and had helped him through his first dangerous days in action. He had become Mannock's protégé, shooting down eight enemy machines in only four weeks. Mannock tried desperately to control his emotions during the party that night but eventually had to retire on the pretext of getting a good night's sleep. "Got to get my beauty sleep for tomorrow. Those sodding Huns are going to pay for it." He walked to his hut and spent most of the night in tears. Pilots in the huts nearby could hear the dreadful wailing coming from his hut, the name of Dolan sounding regularly through uncontrollable spasms of grief.

From that day on, Mannock tightened up the discipline of his flight. He became more critical and watched over the men. One new pilot made the mistake of turning away from a fight and landed to meet a furious Mannock. "You left the flight, just when we were going in." The young pilot paled with fear. He had thought that his retreat would have gone unnoticed. "Well, actually, Captain I . . ." "I won't have that sort of thing in my flight. It puts the others in danger." Mannock's blue eyes looked menacingly at the now quivering man. "It's cowardice, and if I see you do it again, I'll shoot you down myself." At this Mannock turned and slammed the mess door. If the guilty man might have doubted his commander's words, he had but two days to wait for the proof.

Diving to the attack, Mannock noticed the same pilot pulling out of formation and reducing speed. Ignoring the German craft in his sights, Mannock threw his machine into a vertical banking turn and while still in this position, fired over the top wing of the coward. The man soon rejoined the flight, and Mannock returned to the German, whom he sent down to crash. Back at Clairmarais, he landed close to the offending pilot and ran over to his machine. Grabbing the man by his flying-jacket, the fuming Mannock tore at his buttons and ripped away the silver pilot's wings. Turning to another pilot, he said: "Replace these with a nice piece of yellow cloth. You hear me, YELLOW!" The man was later transferred to what Mannock called "a nice cushy billet at home. He'll train other poor sods to take his place. Should be shot or sent to the trenches."

In his growing fury at the death of Dolan, Mannock became ruthless in his dealings with all, especially the enemy. So determined was he to make up for the loss of Dolan by killing every German he came in contact with, he eventually began to take risks and break his own rules of air fighting. Often he had lectured his pilots: "Never follow a Hun down, either the ground-fire will get you or one of his chums will be on your tail while you wait to see the crash."

Two incidents convinced his comrades of Mannock's growing aggression. As one pilot would later put it: "He seemed determined to win the war and kill every German with his aeroplane and machine-gun."

The first instance of Mannock's carelessness was noticed by Major Caldwell. Mannock had just forced down an enemy two-seater, and Caldwell flew alongside him near the ground, thinking that he was going down to determine its position. "The Hun crashed, but not badly, and most people would have been content with this—but not Mick Mannock. He dived half a dozen times at the machine, spraying bullets at the pilot and observer who were still showing signs of life. I flew alongside him shouting at the top of my voice for him to stop."

On 21st May he demonstrated his hatred in a fight with a group of Pfalz Scouts. Engaging the enemy at 12,000 feet, over Kemmel Hill, Mannock flew through the German formation, attacking every machine within striking-distance. Coming up behind one, he shot it to pieces; a second went down out of control an instant later. The third fight was an example of cold, calculated killing, reminiscent of a cat playing with a mouse.

As the main body of enemy scouts had fled, the British flyers stood back to watch Mannock dispatch his victims. He latched onto the Pfalz's tail and followed him around for two or three circuits. The Pfalz pilot then half rolled and dived below Mannock, who followed and opened fire when in line with the fleeing German. Becoming desperate, the Pfalz pilot looped and then put his craft into a spin. Mannock followed and kept up his firing although the Pfalz was positioned below him and totally safe from the SE's bullets. Falling to 4,000 feet, Mannock waited for the Pfalz to flatten out, watching the German's controls for the first sign of an attempt to escape. As the now terrified Pfalz pilot twisted and turned out of the spin, Mannock curved gently to within yards of the machine's cockpit and opened up with a long, withering burst of bullets. The Pfalz immediately went into a vertical dive, its dead pilot slumped over his shattered controls.

Earlier that day, he had sent a Hanover two-seater down to crash, making a total score of four for the day, but he seemed unimpressed. To those who knew him well, his lack of enthusiasm was a clear indication of his wish to avenge Dolan. To those who knew him less well, his parting comment as he walked back to his hut was more than enough to convince them of his hatred. "The swines are better off dead. No bloody prisoners for me."

His reputation as a leader and mentor of novices had spread among the front-line squadrons in a matter of weeks, but now another side of Mannock's character was gaining him yet another reputation, 'Mick' Mannock the ruthless killer—'the Iron Man' some called him.

With his anger at the loss of Dolan nearly spent, the success of his other pilots helped once again to bring forth the more cheerful Mannock that the men of 74 had come to know. In a letter to Jim Eyles he wrote: "Poor old Dolan is gone for good. Any hope we could have held out for him is senseless now. Some of the other boys are doing well in recent weeks. Jones is getting on well and looks like being a 'full-out' type when he gains more experience. Clements is coming on fine, no Huns as yet, but coming on fine."

Mick's enthusiasm at 'Taffy' Jones's success was noticed by Major Caldwell and the others; Caldwell took this as an indication that Mannock's heart was warming once again after his period of vengeful killing, and he suggested a prank to 'wake the boys up'—a suggestion aimed more at Mannock than 'the boys', and it served its purposes. He allowed Mannock to complete his praise of Jones and then took him to one side.

"Look, Mick, I've had an idea. We've got a surplus of oranges, much more than we actually need, and I was thinking of a way to use them up."

Mannock looked puzzled, "But how, I mean . . ."

"Let's do a raid on No. 1 Squadron and wake them up a bit."

Taken completely by surprise, the personnel of No. 1 Squadron stood helplessly and watched 74 Squadron tearing across their field, dropping handfuls of oranges which exploded on the roofs of hangars and, in same cases, on their unprotected heads. Waving excitedly to their comrades on the ground, Mannock and his men turned for home. Within the hour, No. 1 Squadron returned the compliment with a shower of over-ripe bananas.

After this hilarious interlude in the horror of war, Mannock was once more recognizable as his old self. Once again the men of 74 could expect to be greeted by his booming voice as they entered the mess. Landing after a successful fight, he could again be heard celebrating in his previously well known style. As he leapt from his still-moving SE5a, his voice would boom around the field, "Got one of the sods. Sizzle, Sizzle, Wonk."

Mannock's return from his single-handed war of revenge was most noticeable in his revived interest in newly arrived pilots. Mr Clements remembers his approach to discovering the potential of a newcomer:

Selection of pilots was done in the usual manner, tests of their abilities in flying and shooting etc, but Mick had a few non-regulation methods of his own. He was particularly fond of cornering a new boy and describing for him the fall of a burning machine. This was done humorously but in a highly detailed manner. He left none of the gory facts out. If the new boy joined in the laughter, Mick would declare him to be OK. If the chap looked even slightly sick, Mick would keep a more watchful eye on him. He wasn't always as kind to newcomers, although they had to be pretty hopeless for him to reject them.

On one occasion we had a new pilot posted to the flight who had only a few hours of flying-time on SE5 machines. In those days a chap could be sent to the front when he could only just handle a machine, never mind 'stunt' around the sky. We took him up, and things did not go well. It seemed that he had no idea of how to use his throttle to keep in position with the rest of us. One minute he was behind, the next he was tearing past us. He was in the position next to mine, and I had to keep an eye on him, not only for his sake but for my own. Luckily I happened to look over my shoulder in time to see him coming straight up behind me. I half rolled out of the way and recovered in time to see him fly at full speed through the space I had been occupying.

After we had landed, he complained that none of us could fly and that he had been hard pushed to avoid running into us all. Mick listened to him and then took me aside. He said, "Clem, about the new boy. Get him by yourself, take him into one of the huts and shoot him. You got it, shoot him!"

Mick was probably more angry with the training-schools which could pass such inexperienced men for active duty than he was with the new boy. I had a word with the lad, and he went back for further instruction.

Mannock could also be more gentle in his handling of newcomers to the unit. Walking into the mess one day after a patrol, he stopped dead in his tracks at the sight of an incredibly young face at the bar. He had expected a new pilot—but this was a baby. Mannock smiled to conceal his surprise and approached the new man.

"Ah, you'll be the replacement pilot we heard about."

"Sir!"

"I expect you'll be feeling a bit lost, are you, away from home and hearth and all that?"

"Sir!"

"Have a drink, will you?"

"Thank you, sir, er yes. I'll have a Scotch and . . ."

Mannock turned abruptly to the barman, "A large lemonade for our new chap, will you please." At this Mannock laid down his flying-gloves and turned on the young man.

"How old are you?"

Unable to avoid the penetrating stare, the boy stuttered into an answer which he knew was unconvincing as soon as it left his lips.

"Er, I'm—uhm—eighteen, sir, eighteen."

"Are you now? By that I take it you mean seventeen, or is it sixteen?"

Blushing heavily, the new boy's head sank as he admitted,

"Well, I'm actually seventeen, sir, nearly eighteen though."

"Faked your age, did you?"

"Sir!"

"Well, you had better come into 'A' Flight with me. We can keep an eye on you until you're ready to go over the line. I'll fix it up."

A number of young and under-age pilots would come under the searching gaze of Mannock. Their relief at not being sent home soon turned to thankful admiration of this tall, scruffy pilot who had taken an interest in them—more so when they discovered that he was the leading pilot of the unit and was knocking down Germans almost daily. When they later realized that Mannock was giving up his spare time and rest-periods to teach them what he knew of air fighting, their admiration soon turned to outright worship. It became a common sight on the aerodrome, Mannock walking out to a pair of waiting SE5s with a young pilot, his large, bony hands demonstrating what was expected of the beginner. A short time later the SEs would return. Mannock would rarely claim a victory after these training-flights, leaving the new man to file his first combat report and later singing his praises in the mess. In this way Mannock completed the work he had set out to do in 74. Morale was at its highest, the Squadron aggressively cutting into the German Air Force.

So great was the effect of 74 Squadron's actions that the Germans believed 74 to be a handpicked unit commanded by the great McCudden. For Mannock to be compared so favourably with such a successful pilot (for it was certainly he to whom the Germans referred in captured intelligence papers) was the greatest compliment he could have received at that time.

On 24th May a visit from General Plummer threw the Squadron into extensive efforts to clean up their rather untidy quarters. Plummer arrived only minutes before Mannock landed with his flight after a patrol over the lines and watched the planes bounce onto the grass and then pull into their individual places on the flight line. He was the classic example of a staff officer, his uniform perfect in every respect. As the pilots of 'A' Flight jumped down from their machines, he turned to Major Caldwell and asked: "Which is Captain Mannock?" The sight of Mannock caused a look of shock to appear on the General's face. Taffy Jones described Mannock on that day as being "the most disreputable of us all . . . he was hatless, without a collar, his tunic open, his hair ruffled; in fact, he looked a typical bush-ranger!"

Plummer walked over to the grimy figure of Mannock and held out his hand. "Let me congratulate you on your award of the DSO." Smiling broadly, Mannock grasped the shocked little General with his filthy hand and thanked him warmly. Hardly able to believe that this scruffy 'lout' was one of the Air Force's most successful members, Plummer turned away from him and the gathering throng of pilots who ignored the General and approached to shower congratulations on their flight commander.

That night, 74 were joined by 85 to celebrate Mannock's DSO in typical RAF style. Lieutenant Kiddie was present at the party and wrote of it:

It was a great 'do'. 85 were represented by 'Nigger' Horn, Springs, Grider and Artie Daniels. We had speeches galore, and one of our boys, Richardson, who was called 'the Cocktail King', mixed up a vicious brew for our consumption called 'the 74 Viper'. These just about killed poor old Mick, who wasn't much of a drinker, but everyone else liked them. It was one of the few occasions that anyone actually got properly drunk. We didn't drink much as a rule. We were so excited most of the time that one or two would do the trick. But that night was different.

Urged on by this encouraging reward, Mannock went back into fight with renewed energy. H. G. Clements relates the story of Mannock's first fight after the award of his DSO, which also demonstrates the teamwork evident in 74.

On 28th May we were out looking for trouble and soon found it. Near Kemmel we attacked two Pfalz scouts. Mick had already spotted another crowd of Huns preparing to attack but decided to have a crack at the first two before the others could come to their assistance. The first two Pfalz from the top crowd came down rather faster than we had anticipated, and I was almost cut off. Seeing my predicament, Mick pulled them away from me by going underneath them and drawing their fire onto himself. It was a rotten sight to see all those heading for him, and if it had been anyone but him I would have been scared stiff for his safety. Once Pfalz got on his tail, so Mick went down pretending to be out of control. He was doing everything possible, spinning, upside down, everything but bring up his breakfast. This allowed me to get in behind them and give them a few squirts. As they turned on me, Mick flattened out and joined me above the Huns, who were a bit confused by this time. We headed for home, and the Huns must have decided that we were not worth the effort and did likewise.

We then climbed to 10,000 feet and met with Grid, who was also out for some fun. We went back over the line and pounced on two Albratros scouts but once again fell foul of a large bunch of their friends. We fought our way clear, guarding each other all the way. That was the kind of thing that happened with the 74 boys. We were never really trapped by the Huns, but we were chased out of the sky on some of these unofficial patrols in the evenings with Mick. We had a lot of fun as well as frights.

On the following evening, Mannock gave a fine demonstration of his ability. At 7.40 pm, near Armentières, he attacked a two-seater with Clements and Jones and watched it crash heavily to the ground. Noticing a formation of machines in the distance, he flew across to meet them and discovered that they were from 85 Squadron. Waggling their wings at each other, 'Nigger' Horn and Mannock led the combined units on a patrol deep inside enemy territory.

Some 2 miles further inside 'Hunland', they met twelve Albatros scouts. Mannock led the formation in a steep-diving attack on the enemy, charging straight into them with his guns blazing. The German leader broke away from the main body of his flight and came at Mannock— head on. At a combined speed of over 200 miles an hour, the scouts charged at each other. Mannock watched his bullets passing those of the German pilot which came whining past his ears. Flashes on the German's cowling indicated hits on vital spots, but still the Albatros came on. Mannock knew that to pull out would expose him to the German's guns, and he continued his attack. As the German grew to enormous proportions over the nose of the SE, Mannock squeezed himself into as small a target as possible and prayed. With only seconds to spare, the Albatros wheeled over and fell out of the sky, its pilot dead.

Wheeling away from the disintegrating machine, Mannock charged at another and likewise sent it down. He had sent down three enemy craft in under sixteen minutes and could feel the warmth of elation spreading through his veins. He also noticed that his hands were shaking uncontrollably.

On 30th May he was awarded a bar to his DSO, and the flight celebrated the event in style. It was during this celebration that Mannock discussed his health in an uncharacteristically open fashion with Jones. Discarding his usual reserve in such personal matters, he took Jones to one side and sat with his arm around the shoulder of the Welshman who was becoming a close friend.

"Taffy, my nerve is going. Shaking like a leaf most of the time."

"Not you, Mick, you seem well on top of it all."

Mannock's head turned quickly towards Jones, "You mean you can't see it, is that it? As long as none of the boys have noticed, that's what really worries me."

"Why not ask for a rest? You deserve one after all you've done. See Grid about it. He'll fix you up."

"It's because of Grid that I won't ask. I'd feel terrible running off home while he and the rest of you are out here in the thick of it."

6
The Nightmare

Death became the uppermost thought in Mannock's mind. During the hours between patrols, he could be seen alone walking around the aerodrome, searching for some quiet spot where he could be by himself. He had, everyone noticed, become extremely lazy whilst not in the air. If not lying about in the grass fields surrounding Clairmarais field, he would sleep in a corner of the mess, unaware of the noisy 'rags' and games going on around him.

Initially the pilots of 74 found this change in Mannock worrying. He had ceased to join in the mess games and celebrations; even his own successes failed to rejuvenate his formerly irrepressible spirit. Those pilots who tried to approach the immobile Mannock soon learned, however, that he was best left alone with whatever thoughts were occupying him. To those who tried to engage him in conversation, his reaction was frightening: to any form of question or remark, he would show little or no reaction, only looking off into space at some unseen object and then turning slowly to speak in a faint voice: "Those blasted flamers—why no parachutes for us?"

Mannock was becoming more and more obsessed with the thought of going down in flames. For over a year he had managed to control his fear of fire, but now his failing nerves were beginning to bare his tortured soul for all to see. His preoccupation with fire was made worse by the fact that the British High Command had refused to let their pilots carry parachutes, even though German airmen were using them successfully. The RAF pilots became more angry when they read the official reason for their being refused the life-saving equipment.

It is the opinion of the board the present form of parachute is not suitable for use in aeroplanes and should only be used by balloon observers.
    It is also the opinion of the board that the presence of such an apparatus might impair the fighting spirit of pilots and cause them to abandon machines which might otherwise be capable of returning to base for repair.

This insulting statement caused the fighting men at the front to complain greatly against the non-flying officers who had compiled that report; to Mannock it served only to stoke the fires of despondency which were burning deep into his weakening mental stability.

Nightly he would awake from some terrible nightmare, his body soaked in sweat. It was always the same: burning Germans, burning British. The intensity of the dreams increased until he could only dream of his own burning descent. His off-duty hours became similarly filled by the continuous memories of burning machines. In his mind's eye he could still see the burning remains of Lieutenant Skeddon's machine on the aerodrome, still smell the sickening stench of roasting flesh. He had seen his victims and comrades alike dying in the petrol-fed infernos which the highly inflammable machines of the period rarely failed to become. He had seen men jumping from their machines at high altitudes to escape the hungry flames, struggling like blackened dolls to escape the clutches of a flaming death. And then there was always the memory of Frech in his burning DFW.

Only in the air could Mannock find a temporary release from his fear. The concentration required by his job overcame the dreadful images, and he threw himself into this respite with much energy.

On 1st June he had 'A' and 'C' Flights over the lines near Estaires and engaged seven Pfalz scouts. Meeting at a height of 13,000 feet, the opposing formation fell into the deadly, swirling mêlée which fighter pilots dreaded. Every second spent in this type of combat called for the max- imum concentration of each man involved. Seventeen machines occupied a small space in the sky, turning con- stantly to avoid collision with the others, British and German. Only the smallest fraction of a second could be allowed for sighting a foe and firing off a killing burst, for the slightest delay in pulling away from an intended victim would almost certainly bring death.

As often happened in such mass combats, the air cleared in an instant, the disappearance of the enemy coming as a shock to the pilots of both forces. Three of the blue-and- white Pfalzes had fallen from the sky in the brief period of five minutes, all of them to Mannock's guns. One had spun away out of control; one had been seen to crash; the third floated down in a slowly descending ball of fire. Mannock found his gaze fixed on the horrific sight as it spun towards the ground but was distracted by the sight of a rapidly spinning object. From its colouration the machine was obviously an SE5a. Its rate of spinning increased as it fell, tearing off the wings and sending the fuselage down in a vertical nose-dive. Mannock managed to focus his eyes on the falling wreckage and recognized the machine as that of Captain Cairns. He had been much loved in the Squadron, and his death was the signal for each of the SEs to go after the retreating German flyers. Catching them in a matter of seconds, the British 'saw red' and in their orgy of hate failed to hit any of the Pfalz scouts.

Later, back at their home base, the men of 74 watched their commander jump from his machine and head directly to his hut and slam the door. Stripping off his sweat- and oil-stained flying-gear, he felt the rising tide of his nervousness welling up inside his trembling body. His hands shook uncontrollably as if being vibrated by some gigantic device designed for the purpose of tearing his body apart. The dreadful trembling flowed into his legs and arms; even the interiors of his eyes refused to remain still. His pulsating stomach and rapid breathing forced cries from his saliva-flecked lips, tiny, almost inaudible pleas from his tortured mind. Through the rising tide of approaching madness came the sounds of his men returning to their huts to wash off the dirt of combat. A knock at his door brought Mannock out of his spasms in an instant. Jones entered: "Ah—see you in the mess later, Mick. We must give old Cairns a good send-off." Jones watched as Mannock turned away, seemingly occupied with a particularly obstinate button. Without turning around, Mannock replied in a faint voice. "Yes, of course, Taffy. See you all in about an hour."

Later, in the mess, Jones was surprised to see his friend arrive in a manner which none of the pilots had seen for some time. Mannock had obviously spent a great deal of time preparing for the 'celebration', having shaved and changed into one of his less wrinkled tunics. Walking into the mess in his stiff, bouncing gait, Mannock immediately asked for a drink and then joined in the game of mess rugby which was slowly demolishing the aged furniture. Soon he had discarded the tunic and was throwing himself into the proceedings with abandon. He was seen emerging from the bottom of the scrum time after time and jumping back onto the summit of the sprawling mass.

At the end of the game, Mannock was unable to organize yet another round of this rowdy pastime and consented to make a speech before dinner. Rising from his seat at the head of the table, he drew the attention of all present by flashing one of his greatly missed smiles. To each of the men around the table, it was immediately obvious that Mannock had returned to form. They had missed his witty speeches and musical performances in the mess and sat silently awaiting their commander to speak. "Gentlemen, a toast," said Mannock raising a large tankard. "To Captain Cairns—and the last dead Hun. Sod the Huns." Drinking down his beer in large gulps, he then presented them with a speech which all agreed was his best to date.

Calling for silence amid thunderous applause at the end

of his amusing talk, Mannock looked seriously at the assembly. "We have lost some damn good men in this fight of ours against the Huns, but we are giving the bastards hell. They are on the run at last, and that's how they are going to be until we chase them back to Berlin." Pausing for yet another thirsty draw on his beer, Mannock continued with a devilish gleam in his eyes. "I actually believe that some of you are going at the Huns a bit much and would therefore ask you to ease off and leave a few for this old fella."

The dinner continued noisily into the early hours of the morning. Mannock contributed greatly to the evening's entertainment with his songs and violin tunes. It was only when he played his violin that evening that any of the company sensed sadness in his behaviour. Pulling every piece of emotion from the melodies of 'Ave Maria' and the 'Londonderry Air', he held his audience spellbound as they watched his tall, gaunt figure standing in a badly lit corner of the mess. His expressive face added to the emotional music and heightened its effect on the pilots. When told of the quality of his playing and his facial expressions, Mannock refused to play further unless allowed to face the wall.

At the end of a glorious evening, the laughing pilots of 74 walked to their huts happy in the thought that their senior flight commander had returned to his previous high spirits. They discussed his recovery and the reasons for his apparent decline. "He is over thirty years old, you must remember," said one young pilot. "That's only nine or ten years older than most of us, but it must put him under great strain." Before parting, the pilots of Mannock's flight agreed that their flight commander had been suffering from nerves, a condition, they decided, that was only to be expected in a man of his age who had fought so hard and so long. Had they passed Mannock's hut at that moment, their reasoning would have been proved most faulty.

Immediately upon returning to his hut, Mannock had fallen onto his cot. Wrapping his arms tightly around his shaking body, he made a desperate attempt to halt the return of the trembling-spasm. He felt a great guilt at his failure to withstand the strains of the previous months, knowing that any weakness in him would eventually cause the death of one of his men in combat. That, Mannock decided firmly, was not going to be allowed to happen. Whatever the consequences to his own health, his fear would not affect his leadership or be allowed to show in front of the men who depended on him. Forcing the gathering images from his mind, Mannock drew strength from the distant laughter of his men.

To Jones, the only man to whom he had openly confessed his decline, the sight of Mannock on the following morning was gratifying. Once more he was to be seen bouncing across the field with his pilots, their combined laughter only just succeeding in drowning out his happily booming voice. His confessed fear of burning had seemingly disappeared into a complete disregard of the possibility of such a death. As he joined the laughing throng, Jones was further pleased by his jovial nature. Walking with Mannock to the waiting line of SE5s, his pilots were bombarded with a series of jokes concerning which of them would go down in flames first. Drawing their attention to one young pilot who had been plagued with continuous bad luck since his arrival at the front, Mannock announced:

"Now this lad, an absolute hoodoo, a Jonah if I ever saw one. Quicker he gets it in burning bits the better."

Allowing the laughter to subside, Mannock turned his attention on the approaching form of Major Caldwell.

"Morning, Grid. Nice day for it."

"Indeed, Mick. All set are you?"

"Absolutely, but I wouldn't go up today if I were you. No sir."

Caldwell knew Mannock well enough to know what was coming next.

"Saw it all in my dreams last night," continued Mannock giving an exaggerated wink to his men. "Yes, there was Grid's old SE going down, burning good and proper. The only bit that wasn't alight was the tailskid. So Grid, being a sensible sort of chap, was hanging onto it as he floated down. Never mind, Grid, I'll send the bits home to your folks."

Caldwell replied with a similarly imagined dream in which Mannock was going down in flames whilst hanging onto his tailskid. Mannock's laughter was to be heard over that of all as the cheering crowd dispersed towards their machines.

Major Caldwell writes:

> This was the sort of war-going attitude we fostered in 74, an indefinable mixture of aggression, hate and revenge, mixed with a happy feeling of comradeship and not taking things too seriously, at least on the face of it. Mannock was a master at bringing about this necessary state of mind in his followers. It produced results against the enemy and kept everyone happy and as free from the nervous strain of aerial combat as possible.

Waving to the still laughing Major Caldwell, Mannock signalled for the take-off and gunned his SE across the grass and into the air.

At 15,000 feet over German territory, Mannock saw a small cluster of dots which were moving rapidly towards Armentières. Signalling the presence of the enemy to his flight, he slowly manoeuvred the SEs into a position which would prevent the enemy from escaping. Seeing that the time was right for his attack, he wheeled his machine over and into an almost vertical dive. With his airspeed-indicator showing 160 mph, he eased the stick further forward and went straight for the German leader. Still unseen by the enemy flight, Mannock waited until the last possible moment and then pulled sharply out of his dive. As he levelled out, a white-tailed Pfalz appeared in his sights and received fifty rounds through its cockpit at a range of 25 yards. The enemy pilot slumped over dead, and his machine fell spinning to the earth far below.

This fight was a classic example of Mannock's methods in the air. He would spot the enemy aircraft well before they had seen him and then manoeuvre into a position which not only gave him the advantage in attack but would also prevent the Germans from escaping. The long, steep dive at high speed onto his prey was also typical of his style, and the skill required to hit a swiftly moving target from any given angle was something that few pilots could match. Mannock had developed this system of fighting as an answer to his own doubtful abilities which were evident during his first days with 40 Squadron. With 74 Squadron he developed the system to its peak of perfection and adapted it so that even his less talented pilots gained many successes. The undoubted superiority of 74 over their German opponents (and to a large extent over the other Allied units) was due in the main to Mannock's training and the leadership given by him and 'Grid' Caldwell. Even at the peak of his own career, Mannock put the security and improvement of his flight above any ambitions he might justly have had for himself. The fact that his own personal 'score' could have easily been increased beyond that of any other pilot then in the air was forgotten in his desire to make 74 the leading Squadron at the front without suffering large numbers of casualties.

H. G. Clements writes of Caldwell's and Mannock's contributions to the morale of the unit:

They were always up to something or another to keep our spirits up. On one occasion, when we had just landed from a patrol, Mannock came in and immediately attracted our attention.

He flew low over the field, and we could see him in his cockpit clearly. It was a wonderful sight to see. He had discarded his helmet and was lying back in his seat smoking his pipe; he must have lit it up while still over the lines, and the sight of him coming in like that, with his long muffler blowing out behind, was a great 'lift' to us all.

Of Caldwell, Clements writes:

Grid had a great sense of humour and was a grand Commanding Officer. I remember when he came back from leave with an assortment of black, white and ginger false beards. We all wore these during a patrol, and Grid said that the Huns would think the British were using 'old timers' and take us for 'easy meat'. This was all slightly mad, but it was things like this that kept us going and produced the wonderful spirit which one found in 74.

Mannock also returned to his practice of blooding young pilots during June 1918, but his first attempt at this in months was not particularly happy for him.

Lieutenant 'Swazi' Howe was the youngest member of 74. He had enlisted after being rejected for further education in his homeland of South Africa and was only seventeen years old when he first joined in the battle. He was so small that he had trouble in reaching the rudder-pedals in his SE and had to have extra cushions fitted to his seat. Mannock was concerned that Howe was the only member of his flight not to have scored a 'kill' and decided to help the youth.

Taking Howe over the lines to "find some war", Mannock saw six Albatros scouts near Armentières and in the distance a flight of Sopwith Camels. Flying up to the 'Camel' leader, Mannock signalled that he wanted the Camels to assist, and on seeing the other flight leader respond positively, he heeled over and dived on the unsuspecting Germans. Passing through the Albatros formation, he then turned for a second attack and saw to his horror that the Camels had pulled away, leaving Howe and himself to handle six angry Germans. Mannock and his charge only just succeeded in escaping after firing all their ammunition in a desperate dog-fight. On landing, Mannock's machine turned over, due to the fact that his tyres had been torn to shreds by the enemy gunfire. Furiously, he stepped from the upside-down SE and demanded that the Camel leader be court-martialled.

After investigating the event, Caldwell was able to inform Mannock that the Camel flight had broken away to engage another enemy formation which was coming down to attack. Mannock mumbled his disbelief at the news but gladdened when Caldwell also announced that the Camel leader had confirmed that one of the enemy craft had gone down in flames. Mannock immediately called out to 'Swazi' Howe: "Hey, Swazi, you got it. Get a report in." The slightly confused South African walked to the Recording Officer's room to report the combat of which he had little memory.

Mannock's interest in previously successful pupils who had lost their initial confidence was also revived during this period. When 'Taffy' Jones returned from leave on 16th June, he had, he said,

'Not yet recovered my balance, so to speak. When I opened fire the first time, I even jumped with fright at the noise! After breakfast I went up with Mick's patrol. I felt I could do with a little inspiration from him. I was quite frank with him about why I was going up. He laughed and said, "Taffy, old lad, I've often felt like you. Come up with me, and I'll send one down, sizzle, sizzle, wonk. It will just put you right. You can fly on my left. You'll get a better view from there.'

Later, after spotting a German machine and attacking, Jones wrote:

It was a grand sight to watch. There was Mick, just in front of me, doing 180 miles an hour, with the bullets pouring out to the accompaniment of the vicious barking of two machine-guns. At 8,000 feet it was plain that the enemy had bought it. He was going down at a steeper and steeper angle. I pulled out to watch the end. It came in a cloud of dust.

My blood-lust had been re-awakened. My confidence was returning. Good old Mick!

Later that afternoon, Mannock led 'A' and 'C' Flights on what he knew would be his last patrol with 74 Squadron, the official notification of his leave having arrived that morning. Nearing Dickebusch Lake, he spotted a lone Fokker D7 biplane, the latest and most deadly German machine at the front. Signalling Lieutenant Roxburgh-

Smith to follow him, he dived under his own formation and left them to act as decoys upon which the Fokker might be drawn, not realizing that two more SEs were waiting for him below the main group. Seeing that the German pilot was not to be fooled by this ploy, he flew alone to a position in front of and below the Fokker and tried to tempt the enemy pilot into making a move. Eventually the Fokker came down on Mannock in a most timid fashion and was confused by his unconventional behaviour. Hauling heavily on his controls, the British pilot threw his SE around the sky, making it impossible for the enemy to draw a bead on him. While watching the mad antics of Mannock, the German flyer was unaware of Roxburgh-Smith coming from behind. Waiting until the last moment, 'Rox' took careful aim and sent a burst of flaming tracer-bullets into the Fokker. Immediately it reared up and fell away on its back, heading vertically for the ground. The stricken machine then lifted its nose and climbed back towards the SEs in a wide, climbing loop but, on reaching the top of the loop, fell back into the inverted spin to the earth. Seeing that the pilot must have been killed by Roxburgh-Smith's fire, Mannock rejoined the formation and signalled their return home.

The following morning, 18th June, Mannock left his friends in 74 and sailed home for a well deserved leave-period in England.

7
The Premonition

Arriving at the RAF Club in London, Mannock received two yellow envelopes and, hurrying upstairs to his room, slit open the first of them. "Captain Mannock, E, RE att RAF Awarded Bar to DSO." The news of this, his third DSO, had little effect on Mannock; the second envelope, however, had a strong effect on his emotions. After reading the telegram, he crumpled it into a ball and threw it to the floor. Sitting at his table he wrote to Jim Eyles:

18th June

Dear Jim,
Just heard that I've been promoted (Major) and am taking command of Bishop's Squadron in France. I'm not sure that I'm glad of the transfer, as I don't like the idea of leaving my old Squadron, but it can't be helped.
Well, Cheerio.
Pat.

PS. Keep it out of the papers.[1]

Having only two weeks' leave left to him, Mannock went on a tour of his friends and family. At his mother's home in Birmingham he found the scene unchanged from his last visit. The old woman had sunk further into her alcoholic daze. She constantly harangued him about the lack of money sent to her and the little attention paid to her by her children. Could they not remember how much she had

---

[1] Jim Eyles was in the habit of reporting Mannock's successes to the Socialist newspapers of the time. The established Press gave him little coverage, and he was in fact better known in the USA than in Britain.

sacrificed for them, she asked. He remained in his mother's home for what he considered to be a respectable period and then left with all haste for the Eyleses' home in Wellingborough.

To a man in Mannock's state of mind, the arrival at the Eyleses' peaceful home was the opening of his mental floodgates. For months he had bottled up his emotions lest they take command of his senses and become noticed by the other pilots. To his old friend Eyles he poured out all the worries and fears of the past few months. A dutiful and trusty friend, Jim Eyles listened to the painful memories and watched Mannock's face contort as the mental images of past horrors were reborn. Some years later, Jim Eyles wrote of him:

I well remember his last leave. As soon as he entered the house, he changed dramatically. Gone was the old sparkle we knew so well; gone was the incessant wit. I could see him wringing his hands together to conceal the shaking and twitching, and then he would leave the room when it became impossible for him to control it.

As the time for his return to the front came closer, he became a different man. On one occasion we were sitting in the front talking quietly when his eyes fell to the floor, and he started to tremble violently. This grew into a convulsive straining. He cried uncontrollably, muttering something that I could not make out. His face, when he lifted it, was a terrible sight. Saliva and tears were running down his face; he couldn't stop it. His collar and shirt-front were soaked through. He smiled weakly at me when he saw me watching and tried to make light of it; he would not talk about it all. I felt helpless not being able to do anything. He was ashamed to let me see him in this condition but could not help it, however hard he tried.

Later he told me that it had just been a 'bit of nerves' and that he felt better for a good cry. He would not admit that it had been more than 'a cry', and he avoided any further discussions.

When he left our home for the last time, there was some-

thing very wrong. I could feel it. On previous leaves he would
skip out of the front door and talk very quickly and excitedly
about getting back to the war, the next leave and the presents
and souvenirs he would bring back.

But that last leave had something very final about it all.
Pat was a very sensitive chap, and I do feel that he knew he
was saying goodbye. He was in no condition to return to
France, but in those days such things were not taken into
consideration.

Just how much Mannock had hidden his feelings in 74
Squadron can be seen by comparing the report of Jim
Eyles with that of Major Caldwell, the opinions being
formed within two days of each other. Caldwell writes:

I cannot say that at the time I sensed any signs of Mannock
cracking up. He never 'went sick' or asked for time off. When
the Wing Commander, Colonel van Ryneveld, asked initially
if he could have Mannock as CO of 85 Squadron, Mannock
pleaded with me to keep him in 74 so that he could get all the
action possible. He was afraid that the paperwork which a
Commanding Officer was lumbered with would stop him
leading his men and fighting. No sign of nerves there; he was
in perfect health.

Mrs Dorothy Mannock, his sister-in-law, was present at
the party given for him on the eve of his departure for
France, and her memories form a further, rather sad,
picture of 'Mick' Mannock at this time. Although deep in
his thoughts and preoccupied with his return to the front,
he tried his best to reassure his friends and family and
relieve their concern. Knowing of his fine baritone voice,
Dorothy asked him to sing for the company. He responded
with an emotional rendering of a piece from *Faust*, the
most memorable line for Dorothy being: "Even the bravest
heart will swell at the moment of farewell."

Mannock boarded the leave-boat for France on 3rd July
1918. Lying in his cabin, he suffered from sea-sickness, a
condition which increased his misery. His leave had

weakened him considerably, not only in that he had to face up to the horrors contained in his memory but also the physical weakening caused by a severe bout of influenza. He lay back in his bunk and tried desperately to arrange his confusion of thoughts into some kind of order.

Mannock knew that he was in no condition to command a squadron; mentally and physically he was drained beyond the limit of human endurance. His leave had been too short to relieve his obsession with the death which he knew was no more than a possibility. The odds against his surviving a third tour of duty were enormous. He would spend each second of his time at the front waiting for death. Mannock exhausted himself further in his search for a way of overcoming the horror which was growing steadily in his mind and then fell into a feverish dream of burning aircraft.

Arriving in Boulogne the next day, he walked past the transport tender waiting to take him to 85 Squadron and hitched a lift to visit his friends in 74. That night in the company of so many old comrades was too much for his mental stability. Bombarded with their congratulations on his promotion, he broke down and wept in front of them all. But seeing these men with whom he had faced danger so often did bring about a change in his attitude. He had conquered his fear before because of their need of his leadership; now he would have to do exactly the same thing with his new command. Holding back his last tears of sadness, Mannock climbed into the Squadron car the following morning and waved goodbye to his beloved pilots of 74.

85 Squadron, stationed at St Omer, was not at the peak of performance when Major Mannock arrived to assume command on 5th July. It was obvious to him that their morale was extremely low and their need of leadership great. The sight of so many despondent faces gave a much-needed boost to his strength, and he immediately set about recognizing the problems he would have to overcome.

Major Billy Bishop VC, the unit's previous commander,

had belonged to the 'old school' of fighting pilots and be-lieved in flying alone. While Bishop was fighting his lone war far over the lines and increasing his considerable score of enemy machines, the men of 85 had been left to fend for themselves. One of the pilots, 'Nigger' Horn, had managed to organize the unit into some semblance of a fighting squadron, but his lack of experience had pre-vented his completing the task. To the men of 85, the arrival of Mannock was the answer to a prayer. In him, whom they knew from his time with 74, they saw the answer to their problems and a halt to the casualties that had plagued them for so long.

He began his time with the Squadron by carrying out a ruthless purge of the men whom he considered unsuitable. Applying the lessons he had learned in 40 and 74 Squadrons, he went tirelessly from man to man, asking question after question, forming an impression of each pilot's capabilities and aggressive instinct. When he had 'cut out the rot', Mannock was left with an impressive list of pilots which included some names destined to make history: Elliot White Springs, Larry Callaghan, John Grider (three Americans known as 'the Musketeers'), 'Nigger' Horn and McDonald.

Mannock began teaching his methods of team fighting, and within the short period of two days, the previously despondent pilots were eager to cross the lines and try out his tactics. Seeing the change in his men, he called them together for a briefing.

"When we go out, I shall take three of you with me to act as decoys. The rest of the flights will follow in two layers above. I shall give the signal to attack—but they must not attack before I give that signal." Pointing to 'Nigger' Horn, he continued. "You, with McGregor and Callaghan and Inglis, will form the top layer. You, Randall, will have the remaining three with you in the middle."

That evening, at 8.20 pm, Mannock spotted the enemy over Doulieu and prepared his flock for combat. Ten Fok-ker D7s approached and then divided, five of them rocketing down on Mannock while the remaining five stood off to await Randall, who was attacking after seeing Mannock's signal. As the German and British flights met head on, 'Nigger' Horn and his men came tearing down from above and sealed the Fokkers in a deadly trap. As the swirling dog-fight descended from 16,000 to 2,000 feet, five of the black-and-red Fokkers fell out of control. Mannock hit two, Horn two and Longton one.

Returning to their home field, the SE pilots found that they had suffered no casualties and that their machines had suffered little damage from enemy fire.[2] Crowding around Horn, they excitedly discussed the fight and described with much delight the falling German machines. Suddenly they noticed Mannock and fell quiet. Watching their new commander walking across the field, each of them was filled with admiration. This one man had transformed the unit in the short period of two days, and their gratitude was boundless. Driven on by the enthusiasm of his men, Mannock began his training of them in earnest. As with 74, he would call his pilots together after each fight and discuss in detail each of their actions, giving advice to each pilot as required.

So involved with his training-programme did Mannock become that his own score against the enemy failed to increase for a time. Concentrating on obtaining 'kills' for his unblooded pilots and protecting them from attack, he failed to shoot down any Germans for periods up to a week. Feeling at ease with his new role as teacher rather than a fighter, he became settled and more at ease than he had ever been previously. The dreams and tensions which had torn at him for so long disappeared, and a new Mannock was to be seen. This phase of happiness was doomed to last only a matter of days, however.

On 10th July Mannock received the news that his old friend James McCudden had been killed in a flying-accident. Taking off, he had stalled and fallen to the ground, being killed instantly. As the immediate horror of

[2] One pilot had his hand grazed by a bullet.

his friend's death melted away, it was replaced with a yet greater horror. Mannock once more realized his own mortality, and no amount of encouragement from his comrades would prevent his slipping back into his previous depression. To his pilots, the change in their leader was immediately obvious: the 'Iron Man' was breaking down. Once again he became the neurotic depressive, concerned only with killing Germans and avenging the death of his beloved McCudden. The fact that McCudden had not died at the hands of the enemy was irrelevant to the crumbling mind of 'Mick' Mannock.

He began taking enormous risks in combat, going down after enemy machines to spray their already dead crews with yet more bullets. After placing his men in a position which would ensure their success in an attack, Mannock would head off on his own, charging at every German machine in sight. Going up to point-blank range, he would tear the enemy machines to shreds and then follow them down to vent his hatred on the burning remains of his victims. Between patrols, he would take off alone and fly many miles behind enemy lines searching for more victims.

After a week of hysterical destruction, Mannock seemed to calm down once more, but his return to his former self was only partial. He had become preoccupied with the neatness of his dress, taking care to comb the once unruly mop of hair and polishing the age-old dust from his boots. His uniforms were cleaned and decorated with the medal ribbons he had so long neglected. He talked openly and calmly about his now strong premonition of death, telling friends that he was approaching "something final". He continued scoring against the enemy but became even more lax in his reporting of combats. The training of new pilots filled more and more of his time, and it is likely that many of his successes went their way. Mannock felt that he had given his all, and now all that remained was his Squadron and that "something final".

The depressions and high points which had been part of

his life for so long now became more extreme and more
regular. Within the space of a few minutes he would move
from the happy, gay, entertaining wit to the distant depressive involved only with thoughts of his own death. His
depressions, weighed down by the memory of dead friends,
greatly outweighed the effects of happier occasions, and
this, combined with the daily stress of leadership, could
have but one end. To Mannock, who rejected any sugges-
tions of a rest-period, death or total breakdown seemed the
only possible result; death was foremost in his mind.
Avoiding the extreme carelessness which had killed so
many leading pilots after their days of continual success,
he came to accept death as the only logical end to his career
and spent his days waiting for it.

In his last letter home, he wrote: ". . . I feel that life is not
worth hanging on to . . . had hopes of getting married,
but . . .?"

On the morning of 19th July he took off with his men on
patrol and found an Albatros two-seater near Estaires.
Moving into position, he left the flight behind and dived to
meet the German head-on. At the last moment he fired
both guns at point-blank range and killed the enemy
observer. Diving under the damaged machine, he turned
for a second burst and sent the German down in flames. On
the following day he sent two more enemy aircraft down
within a period of an hour, the first a two-seater which
crashed out of control and the second a Fokker scout which
went down trailing smoke.

Phoning 'Taffy' Jones to announce the two victories,
Mannock chided him about his lack of success in the previous weeks and encouraged him to "pull his socks up".

On the evening of 24th July Mannock received a telephone call from 'Taffy' Jones, now the commander of Mannock's old flight in 74 Squadron. Announcing proudly that
he had shot down two Germans, Jones was pleased to hear
Mannock's laughing voice over the crackling line: "Good
man, Taffy. Come over and have lunch and tea with me

tomorrow, and you can explain your methods." "Silly ass!"
replied Jones to his friend's friendly sarcasm. Still laughing loudly, Mannock continued, "I shot a triplane's tail off
over Lille the other day. I've caught up with Bishop's score
now—seventy-two." Answering that there would be a red-
carpet reception awaiting Mannock after the war, Jones
was suddenly met with a long silence which ended with
Mannock saying, in the quietest of voices,

"There won't be any 'after the war' for me, Taff."

"Now stop that, Mick, that's enough!" The line went
dead.

The following afternoon, Jones and Clements arrived to
have lunch with Mannock at 85 Squadron's mess and
noticed immediately that he was in a strange mood. No
longer was he the energetic man they had known so well in
74. Gone was the rapid speech and the hilarious rapport.
Mannock announced happily that the Squadron was doing
well since he had taken over and that they were "kicking
hell out of the Huns", but in the next instant he seemed far
away and unaware of their presence.

Later in the afternoon, a car approached containing two
nurses from the local field hospital. At this Mannock ran
off towards his hut and returned seconds later wearing a
new tunic. One of the nurses was introduced as Sister
Flanagan, and Jones and Clements could easily see that
the nurse meant a great deal to the now beaming Mannock. Joined by some of his pilots, the gathering developed
into a party, and Mannock once more showed the happier
side of his personality which up to then had not been
evident. Jones and Clements put it down to the presence of
the pretty nursing sister and smiled knowingly at each
other.

The party continued happily until Jones mentioned the
subject of a German machine he had burned that morning.
The assembly fell silent as Mannock leaned across to
Jones: "Did you hear the swine screaming at you, Taff?"
Having expected his old teacher to congratulate him in his
usual fashion, Jones was taken aback and looked search-

ingly at Mannock. "That's the way they'll get you if you're not careful, young lad. Anyway, when it comes, don't forget to blow your brains out—you won't notice the difference anyway, Taffy." At this remark, the company burst into peals of laughter—laughter which died quickly as Mannock described the sight of a burning aircraft. Listening to the gory description, Clements and Jones watched their friend's darting eyes turn fiery as he looked into empty space, watching the terrible end he just described.

Shaking his head to rid himself of the dreadful thoughts, Mannock apologized for his morbid speech and then turned to one of his pilots.

"Have you got a Hun yet, Inglis?"

"No, sir, I haven't," admitted the embarrassed New Zealander.

"Well, come on out and we'll get one for you." Taking Inglis by the arm, Mannock turned to his guests and asked, "Will you excuse us for a few minutes, please?"

Walking towards two waiting SEs, Mannock talked rapidly to the young pilot, explaining what would be required of him when they crossed over the lines. Illustrating the last few details with sweeping movements of his hands, he then patted Inglis on the back and headed towards his machine.

The quiet of the day was broken as Mannock ran his engine up to maximum revolutions and shouted to his mechanics to stand clear. In a cloud of dust, he gunned the SE down the landing-strip and took off into the air. Meanwhile Inglis had discovered a fault in his aircraft and had to signal Mannock that he was unable to take off. Rolling his wings to show his understanding, Mannock banked sharply and began his climb towards the lines. Over two hours later, the dismayed Inglis was pleased to hear the sound of his commander's machine coming in to land. When Mannock was told of the fault in Inglis's SE, he reprimanded the ground crew and then turned to the young pilot. "Don't worry, lad. See to your machine—

especially the guns, and we can be off before dawn tomorrow."

Joined by 'Taffy' Jones as he entered his hut to change out of his heavy flying-clothes, Mannock proceeded to curse the lack of Germans in the sky that day. "Did my damnedest to get my seventy-third, but there wasn't one to be seen. I think they've all gone home."

Remembering his friend's strange behaviour that day, Jones asked Mannock how he was feeling. The frank answer was more revealing than Jones had expected.

"I don't think I'll last much longer, Taffy. It's on the cards."

Suddenly Mannock turned and put his long bony hands on the Welshman's shoulders, and with watering eyes said in a broken voice: "Old Taff, if I am killed, I shall be in good company. I've done my duty as best I could."

Changing back into his new tunic, Mannock took Jones by the arm and headed back towards his other guests. Jones felt better as he listened to his friend's cheerful voice as they walked towards Clements and Sister Flanagan. "Rule Britannia, Britannia rules the waves."

8
26th July 1918

That morning, Donald Inglis had risen early from a broken sleep. Through the hours of darkness he had waited impatiently for the time when he would finally make his trip over the German lines with Major Mannock. How good it felt to have this master of the game taking an interest in him, a small cog in the huge wheel of international war, but that, thought Inglis, was one of the things which made Mannock great. How he had changed the Squadron with his wonderful personality and energy! At times Inglis had felt left out of it all, as the more successful pilots in the unit had crowded round their leader and made it impossible for him to be seen. But now he was to have the Major to himself for a private lesson in the art of air fighting. The happiness he felt at the thought of this coming experience made Inglis fully aware of the reason for the unit's hero-worship of Mannock, the effect of his magic. Looking at his wrist watch, he waited for the hands to show 4.30 am and then ran out of his hut.

Slowing his pace down to a walk, Inglis recovered his breath and headed for the old iron hut that the Squadron used as a mess; there, waiting for him, would be Mannock. As he came closer to the mess, Inglis stopped to listen to the sounds issuing from the windows cut in the hut's metal sides. The scratchy sounds of the 'Londonderry Air' flowed from the old Decca gramophone, a sure sign that Major Mannock was waiting for him.

Inglis entered without Mannock's noticing his arrival. He was sitting with his feet resting on a table, smoking the long-stemmed pipe that had become one of his trademarks. As the record came to an end, Mannock turned to play it again and then noticed Inglis standing quietly in the doorway.

"Come in, Kiwi, come on in."

"I'm not late, sir. I made sure that I'd make it on time."

Mannock waved the anxious young pilot to a chair at his side and outlined his plan for their patrol.

"We will head up the lines to see if we can spot one of their two-seaters that come over in the early hours of the morning to spot our guns and shoot up the infantry. Follow my movements exactly and stay close behind on my left. I'll waggle my wings when I'm going to change course and point out any Huns I see." Holding his hands out flat before him, Mannock instructed Inglis in how he should fire at an enemy should they find one: "If he's a two-seater, come in close behind and underneath. I'll have gone in first, so you should get a good idea of what it's all about. Don't fire until your sights are dead on, then give him all you've got."

Smiling at the beaming pilot, he picked up his gloves and strode towards the door. Walking silently at Mannock's side, Inglis watched his commander's face turning as he examined the sky and then looked around the field at the surrounding countryside. As the first streaks of sunlight pierced the haze which hung on the horizon, Mannock drew his comrade's attention to the birds which were singing to welcome the sun. "Do you hear that bird? He's wishing us luck. Full of the joy of life he is. Come on, lad, the mechanics are waiting."

Wishing each of his ground-crew "Good morning", Mannock swung nimbly up onto the edge of his cockpit and then slipped down into the snug pilot's seat. Checking their controls and engines, the two pilots waved to each other and took off into the rising sun.

At 30 miles to the east of St Omer, two German airmen were carrying out a similar process. Leutenant Schopf and Sergeant Hein settled into their craft and headed West towards the British lines.

Some three hours later the pilots of 85 Squadron had risen to prepare for their first patrol of the day. They were more excited that morning than they would normally have been, for they were waiting for the return of their Major and his pupil. Sitting around the Decca gramophone, the pilots read through the mess collection of months-old magazines and chatted optimistically about the probable success of young Inglis. Still laughing at a joke which Grider was in the middle of telling, 'Nigger' Horn walked over to the ringing telephone and lifted the receiver.

"Hello, is that No. 85 Squadron?"

"Yes, this is Captain Horn speaking."

"This is the Archie Battery near Hazebrouck speaking. Has Major Mannock returned?"

"No. Why?"

"Well, a couple of SEs, one of which had a red streamer on its tail and was flown just as Major Mannock usually flies, attacked a Hun about 5.30 am and shot it down in flames; they followed it near the ground, and we have not seen them return; it looked as if they might have been shot down themselves. We are sure it was Mannock because we know his tactics."

Most of the assembled pilots were frightened by this news but refuted its accuracy, saying that the Archie Battery could not possibly recognize Mannock by his flying. Thirty minutes later the most vociferous critics were rendered silent by the sight of a pale-faced messenger. Reading the crumpled note, Horn's face fell to his chest, tears running down to fall on the dusty floor. Taking the note from his hand, another pilot read the message aloud, his voice trembling with shock: "Major Mannock down by machine-gun fire from ground between Calonne and Lestremme after bringing EA two-seater down in flames at Lestremme. Lieutenant Inglis shot through petrol-tank landed on front line at St Floris."

When the news reached the men of 74 Squadron, most of the pilots volunteered to fly over and search for signs of their beloved Mannock. Major Caldwell refused their applications and called 'Taffy' Jones to follow him to the flight line. Caldwell writes of that day: "Taffy and I did try to locate Mannock's crash soon after we were told of his going down. I think we just wanted to see for ourselves that it was over for him and also as a farewell gesture. We saw nothing, and as there was some very heavy ground fire, we had to return."

To the men who had known and loved Mannock during his time at the front, the news was so shocking that they refused to believe it even after the fact became irrefutable. Clements sat alone and thought of the last time he had seen his friend. The image of Mannock sitting in his SE, with his lucky charm of a lady's silk stocking blowing back in the slip-stream, was too much for the young pilot, and he joined the others in their grief.

'Taffy' Jones retired to his hut and wrote in his diary: "26th July—Mick is dead. Everyone is stunned. No one can believe it. I can write no more today. It is too terrible. Just off with Grid to 85 to try to cheer the lads up."

Not even Mannock's closest friends could face up to the full tragedy that had befallen them, but for Donald Inglis it was impossible to suppress the full horror of his Major's death. He had watched the event from a distance of less than 100 yards and would never fully recover from the shock of his experience.

Neither Mannock's aircraft nor his body was ever found, but we do know that someone went to the site of his crash and buried his remains. That unknown German also stripped Mannock of his personal possessions and later sent them via the German Red Cross to Paddy Mannock in England. These sombre relics lay in store for some years until Paddy could stand their presence no longer. Today they lie in an Edinburgh rubbish-dump with only Mannock's identity-disc surviving to tell the tale.

In July 1919 the *London Gazette* announced the posthumous award of the Victoria Cross to Mannock. "This highly distinguished officer, during the whole of his career in the Royal Air Force, was an outstanding example of fearless courage, remarkable skill, devotion to duty and self-sacrifice, which have never been surpassed."

9
'Unknown British Aviator'

Towards the end of July 1918, King George V stood in a
reception room at Buckingham Palace, in his hand a small
black leather-covered case. Opening the case, the King
looked admiringly at the contents: The Victoria Cross, the
Distinguished Service Order with two bars and the
Military Cross with one bar. Closing the case reverently,
the old King handed it to the middle-aged man who had
come to receive it on behalf of the long dead Major Mannock. It was Corporal Mannock. The wily man who had
deserted his family so long ago had reappeared to collect
the medals his son had died for. Expressing his regrets to
the apparently grief-stricken Corporal, the King could
have little idea that Mannock had stipulated in his service
Will that his father should receive nothing from his estate.
Mannock had kept his hatred of his father alive until the
end.

After the presentation, the Corporal disappeared and
the medals with him, but some years later Paddy Mannock
traced them. The woman whom his father had married
bigamously parted with the decorations for the sum of £5;
she too had been deserted by the Corporal. Today they
hang in a place of honour in the Royal Air Force Museum
at Hendon.

Mannock was not forgotten by the friends he had made
during his life. The award of the VC had come only after a
long campaign by his friends to bring his deeds to the
attention of the Minister for Air, Winston Churchill. In
Wellingborough, Jim Eyles had started another personal
campaign . . . On the day of Mannock's death, Jim Eyles

had been sitting in his living-room when a book fell from
its place on the shelf for some unknown reason. At that
moment, Eyles was overcome by the feeling that his friend
was dead. Later investigations showed that the time of
Mannock's crash coincided with the instant that the book
had fallen to the floor.

Desperate for news of Mannock's fate, Eyles began a
series of letters to the Imperial War Graves Commission,
begging for information concerning the final resting-place
of 'Mick' Mannock. For over twenty years he constantly
bombarded the Graves Commission with letters, but
always the reply came back: "I am directed to inform you
that Major E. Mannock VC DSO MC is reported to have
been buried at a point 300 metres north-west of La Pierre-
au-Beure in the vicinity of Pacaut, east of Lillers. I regret,
however, to say that the officers of the Graves Registration
Units have not yet been able to find the grave." Later
inquiries by Eyles brought similar results and eventually
he was forced to abandon his hopes of finding his old
friend's grave. Mannock was listed officially along with
the thousands of dead soldiers who had no known resting-
place, their bodies hidden by the shells which lacerated
the muddy battlefields of the Great War. His name was
carved on the Arras Memorial along with those of other
great airmen whose bodies were never found: Hawker,
Rhys Davids and hundreds of others. At this, the investigations came to a halt, and the facts concerning Mannock's
death and subsequent burial have been lost to history—
until now.

Recent research has produced a set of facts which point
clearly to the location of Mannock's grave and clarify the
actions which brought about his death. By sifting through
the many conflicting reports and checking each piece of
information, a more logical picture of his fate comes to
light.

Two reports exist concerning Mannock's fatal crash:
that of Lieutenant Donald Inglis who flew with him on
that day, and that of Private Edward Naulls who wit-

nessed the action from the trenches occupied by the Second Essex Regiment. First we shall examine the report given by Lieutenant Inglis.

My instructions were to sit on Mick's tail and that he would waggle his wings if he wanted me closer. I soon found that I didn't have much chance of looking around, as Mick would waggle, and the only thing I could do was to watch his tail and stick tight, as he was flying along the lines at about 30 to 50 feet up and not straight for more than a few seconds, first up on one wing tip and then the other. Suddenly he turned towards home, full out and climbing. "A Hun," I thought, but I was damned if I could see one; then a quick turn and a dive and there was Mick shooting up a two-seater. He must have got the observer, as, when he pulled up and I came in underneath him, I didn't see the Hun shooting. I flushed the Hun's petrol-tank and just missed ramming his tail as it came up when the Hun's noise dropped. Falling in behind Mick again, we did a couple of turns over the burning wreck and then made for home. I saw Mick start to kick his rudder and realized we were fairly low, then I saw a flame come out of the side of his machine; it grew bigger and bigger. Mick was no longer kicking his rudder; his nose dropped slightly, and he went into a slow right-hand turn round, about twice, and hit the ground in a burst of flame. I circled at about 20 feet but could not see him, and as things were getting pretty hot, I made for home and managed to reach our outposts with a punctured petrol-tank.

Although this is basically accurate, it fails to give any locations, and has to be read with some suspicion. Inglis had served with distinction in the Army previous to joining the RAF, but as a flyer he was inexperienced, and his report must be viewed as that of an excited and shocked young man. He failed to identify the type of German machine he had engaged, although it was an all-metal, low-wing monoplane, a most unusual type at the front. Checking Inglis's report against the known facts, it is only safe to consider his information as valid up to the point when he mentions Mannock being hit.

The report of Private Naulls is an accurate account of events after Mannock's machine was hit. He states:

> ... [Mannock and Inglis] engaged the Jerry in combat. A few bursts from their guns sent it crashing in flames at Lestremme behind Pacaut Wood. Mannock then dived at about 40 feet. The remaining trees in Pacaut Wood were of varying heights, the tallest about 30 feet; Mannock's aircraft cleared them by a few feet. Inglis circled at about 100 feet.
>
> Suddenly there was a lot of rifle-fire from the Jerry trenches, and a machine-gun near Robecq opened up, using tracers. I saw these strike Mannock's engine. A blueish-white flame appeared and spread rapidly; smoke and flames enveloped the engine and cockpit. His aircraft, the propeller still spinning slowly and making smoke-rings, made a right-hand turn and came towards our line, but, just short of our line, it turned left and back towards Pacaut Wood and went down in a long glide over the trees and beyond, gradually losing height until it hit the ground in the direction of Merville.

Map No. 1 shows the course followed by Mannock and Inglis. From Mannock's flight path, it would appear that he was still alive and not killed by ground-fire as a number of historians have stated. If Mannock had been killed outright by ground-fire, or if he used his revolver on himself, he would not have been able to manoeuvre in such a fashion; any uncontrolled movements at such a low altitude would have sent him immediately into the ground. It would seem reasonable to assume then that he was still alive and manoeuvring his machine in a desperate fight against the flames.

What happened in the last few seconds before the impact, and what subsequently happened to Mannock's body, have remained mysteries from that day. All that was known was that Mannock was reported as having been buried "At a point 300 metres north-west of La-Pierre-au-Beure on the road to Pacaut"—this report emanating from the German Red Cross. Recent investigation of the Graves Commission records can cast some further light on the subject, however.

The exact wording of the German report concerning the location of Mannock's grave was: "300 metres north-west of La-Pierre-au-Beure on the road to Pacaut." An examination of Map 2 will show that this cannot possibly be correct. Pacaut is east of La-Pierre-au-Beure, and any bearing of north-west from La-Pierre-au-Beure does not intersect with a "road to Pacaut". Accepting that the bearing is wrongly translated from the original German report, and substituting east for west in the compass bearing, an interesting picture emerges, as Map No. 2 also shows.

The following points should be noted:

1. The area around point '1' was searched extensively after the war, but no unidentified bodies were found. If the Germans had buried Mannock at this point, they would have had to carry his body for hundreds of yards *towards* the British lines.
2. The aircraft found at point '2', which was destroyed by fire, was the only British machine to fall in this area. This is confirmed by both British and German records. It also coincides with the approximate position of Mannock's crash.
3. The body of the "unknown British flying officer" found at point '4' had been stripped of his personal effects and identification-discs.

From this information it is more than reasonable to assume that the body found at point '4' is that of Mick Mannock and that the aircraft in question was his. The details which would fully substantiate this assumption have unfortunately been lost forever. The serial numbers of the aircraft's engine, and that of its guns, and the physical description of the body, have been discarded at some point in time. Substantial as this evidence may be, it raises further questions. Firstly, how did Mannock's body arrive at a position some 250 yards from the wreck of his machine? Did he jump at the last moment, or was he carried away, still alive, from the burning SE5a? The possibility that he died in the blaze can be discarded. If he had been in the aircraft as it exploded and burned, his body and effects would have been almost completely destroyed, but the slight damage suffered by his notebook, revolver and identification-discs is minimal. Although the notebook was thrown away by his family many years ago, they clearly remember that it was "only very slightly browned on the edges of the pages". The identity-discs are almost as new and show no signs of having been burned.

Whether Mannock jumped from the blaze or was thrown clear and then carried towards a point where he then died, we shall never know. That mystery can be answered only by the German soldier who buried him.

In the Military Cemetery at Laventie, not far from the site of Mannock's crash, lies a grave marked: "Grave 12, Row F, Plot 3. Unknown British Aviator."

Epitaph

No collection of words, however well arranged, can act as an epitaph to Edward 'Mick' Mannock. Even the Victoria Cross Citation ("This highly distinguished officer . . . an oustanding example of fearless courage . . . devotion to duty which has never been surpassed . . .") is yet another example of official cant, empty of Mannock's zeal, hatreds and loves, his visions of a better world. A many-faceted character, Mannock is almost indescribable, even by those who knew him well.

Many of the problems which arise during an examination of 'Mick' Mannock's life are due to the mass of conflicting information which exists, most of which comes from the people who actually knew him. Even after many years of research by a number of historians, he still remains an enigma to an extent, but an examination of the existing studies of his life shows why this is so. Writers have either concentrated on the shy, sensitive side of Mannock, the half blind boy or the fiery Irishman, never on all of these parts of the whole. These one-sided studies have led to a total misconception of an already complex personality, but if we look at all the information and concentrate on no one side at a time, a more reasonable and accurate picture emerges.

That Edward Mannock was born with a great spirit and natural intelligence is undeniable. The qualities he was to display during his short life could not have been manufactured over the years. In the suppressive atmosphere of his early life, he had no opportunities to dissipate his vast store of energy openly and could only withdraw into his mind and await an opportunity which would realize his massive potential. Although he appeared to be a quiet, unassuming child, his mind boiled with frustrated energy. He was looking for an outlet, but outlets appeared only during times of crisis and despair.

The desertion of his father provided the first opportunity for Edward to shine. He could then play a positive part in his family's life, and he threw himself into this task with much vigour. He would return to his mother after a day of back-breaking labour, his undernourished body exhausted, but the fact that he had helped in some way to alleviate the family's poverty was reward enough. The smallest opportunity to take part in life and to succeed in some way brought forth extreme enthusiasm from Edward, but the first sign of rejection would send him back into his introverted ways. His life after the desertion of his father follows a distinct pattern, a base-line of introverted existence punctuated by displays of energetic outbursts. He never went into anything in a half-hearted manner, always his maximum physical and mental effort or nothing at all. He never had the chance to come out of his shell totally; even his civilian and military successes provided him with plenty of cause to retire into his protective mantle.

It is sad to reflect that the most successful period in Mannock's life lasted only just over a year and culminated in his death. In that short space of time he became the most capable of air fighters and tacticians. Modern air-fighting tactics owe much to his teaching, and the great spirit found in the Royal Air Force of today is due to the example of Mannock and his contemporaries.

What Edward Mannock might have become, had it not been for the outbreak of the Great War and his subsequent enlistment, is a matter for conjecture. Many of his friends were convinced that he would have made a great success of a career in politics. Some even go as far as saying that his abilities as an orator, and his desire to improve the lives of the ordinary people, would have made him a first-class Socialist Prime Minister, one who might have changed the course of Socialism in Britain.

What we do know is that the war gave him the opportunity to use his massive potential. His unconventional character and determined ways made him a natural for the air service, where he had the freedom to develop. But, as with all the other periods in his life, there were serious drawbacks. Although he revelled in his new-found life and its hard work, the failures and deep depressions would only grow to match his happiness in success. His sensitive nature had previously required only a small amount of pain to drive him into a depressed state, but the pain grew to massive proportions with the death of a comrade or the horrific sight of a burning aircraft. Mannock's immense energy made him a successful fighter, but his early years of mental seclusion made him far too sensitive for the daily butchery of the Western Front. Active service did not allow a man to show his feelings, and so Mannock had to bottle them up in his increasingly tortured mind. Only on leave could he release these pent-up tortures, his short periods of rest being filled with uncontrollable outbursts which burned deeply into his emotional stability. In wartime, his previously protective tactic of keeping his feelings to himself stripped his soul bare and left him unprotected against the trials he experienced daily. His introverted nature and his ability to hide his mental state from others are probably the cause of so many conflicting views regarding his make-up. No one person, with the possible exception of Jim Eyles, ever knew 'Mick' Mannock well enough to see the mass of conflicting fears, hates, hopes and joys. While relating what they believe to be true, even his closest friends have helped to obscure his true personality and opened up the way for legend. What is left of Mannock's memory is shrouded in the mysteries of the 'Ace with One Eye', the 'Mad Irish Daredevil', etc.

The legend that he was blind in one eye deserves examination. Major Caldwell writes: "He was supposed to be blind in one eye, and one eye did look a bit different, but his sight was excellent. To be such an excellent shot, his sight must have been first class." Mannock's family, who have never been pleased by the handling of his story, can cast more light on this common quoted 'fact': "He did as a child suffer from a serious eye-infection in India which deprived him of his sight for a time, but this was definitely not permanent. His sight was no worse than most people's; in fact it was much better than average. This factor has been picked up and used by writers in their books; perhaps it makes for an interesting title." The last word concerning Mannock's eyesight goes to H. G. Clements, his wingman and close friend: "I have never believed that he was blind in one eye and knew nothing about it until I read about it in one of the books. If you had seen what he could do with a machine-gun to a speeding, twisting Hun, you wouldn't believe it either."

Towards the end of his life, the opposing sides of Mannock's nature began to come together. His drive to succeed in the air receded as he had done all that was possible. He slowly came to terms with his fears and depressions, but only because he deeply believed that both they and his life were about to run their course.

Mannock's prophecies regarding his own death, and that of certain of his comrades, imparts to him a certain mysticism. The fear of burning to death was one common to all except the insensitive and the unimaginative, so we might well ask if Mannock's preoccupation with fire was in any way special. He told McScotch that he had 'feelings' or psychic insights regarding his own fate and that of others, but at the same time we must appreciate that Mannock was a very highly strung and sensitive man, and it may have been this, rather than a psychic gift, that makes his fear of burning appear greater than that of others. It should be stated, however, that Mannock was completely accurate in his prophecies of doom, with regard not only to his own fate but to that of a number of comrades. Whatever his source, Mannock is all the more remarkable because he went on fighting when definitely convinced of his fate.

His death was probably a greater blow to the RAF than was that of von Richthofen to the Germans. Mannock was loved by his men in the true sense of the word, not only as a leader and fighter but as a man in his own right. To many of them he became an almost superhuman figure, and many refused to accept his death even after the fact became irrefutable. No one in the Squadron could bring himself to hold a farewell 'binge' for their dead leader. That one man could achieve this reaction from other men in such a short period of time is almost unbelievable and a greater tribute to 'Mick' Mannock than his 'score' or array of decorations.

Official recognition of Mannock's abilities and achievements came slowly, and even up to the present time they have never been fully recognized. In a country where military tradition is so strongly observed and protected, it seems strange that the present-day RAF pays little attention to one of its greatest members.[1] Young people entering the service today can complete their training and yet hear nothing of this great airman who left them such a rich legacy. The Air Force would do well to emulate their former German enemies. The Jagdgeschwader Richthofen still exists in that country to this very day, as an example to young German airmen for all time.

The books by 'Taffy' Jones and 'McScotch' have at least attempted to make the name of Edward Mannock known to the general public, but even today, when interest in that far-off war is increasing, most people have little or no idea who he was. With little official recognition, Mannock seems to have faded into the background against which we see the brightly painted legends of less worthy men.

Today there are few of Mannock's friends alive to tell the tale. McScotch and Blaxland died in 1962 and 1979 respectively. 'Taffy' Jones went on to fight in the Second World War and then to a writing career in the company of Dylan

[1]The Royal Air Force have a VC10 named in honour of Mannock.

Thomas, but then he suffered a stroke and died as the result of a household accident in 1960. Of Mannock's close friends in 74 Squadron, only two survive, the last remaining members of the original unit.

'Grid' Caldwell, now retired as an Air Commodore in New Zealand, is still actively involved in assisting those who would study that first war in the air. Without his dedicated help and comprehensive knowledge, few aero-historians would get very far.

'Clem' Clements lives quietly near Leicester with his wife, Alice, and has assisted a number of historians with his highly accurate memories of the war and the famous personalities whom he met during those adventurous days. To listen to 'Clem's' memories is to be transported back in time. The years slip away, and one is immediately aware of the great spirit of comradeship and adventure which was experienced by those early fighting pilots. As he speaks of Mannock, the full extent of the man's almost magical power over young pilots like Clements becomes instantly obvious. To see this old gentleman's eyes light up at the mention of his long-dead hero is to see living testimony of Mannock's great spirit. A framed portrait of the man to whom he owes so much is still one of his most cherished possessions.

Mannock, I am sure, would not have cared about the lack of official recognition, but would he have liked the title of 'King of the Air Fighters' as his epitaph? If this title means that he was the top killer in the first aerial war, and that the number of men killed by him are his passport to greatness, then I think not.

If a Valhalla exists, and Mannock would surely be a member, I feel that he would be more pleased with the following comment of Keith Caldwell. Caldwell talks of Mannock's skill in the air and then continues:

... but other things go to make greatness, such as leadership, morale-building, selflessness, comradeship, cheerfulness, in- dividuality and many other virtues which Mick Mannock possessed in full. He was not only the outstanding pilot of World War One but a man in the full sense of word, much older than he should have been for the stresses he bore, a warm, lovable individual, of many moods and characteristics, and I will always salute his memory.

Decorations Awarded to the
Late Captain (Acting Major)
Edward Mannock, RAF

Military Cross
Gazetted 17th September 1917
Temporary Second Lieutenant E. Mannock, Royal
Engineers and Royal Flying Corps.
*"In the course of many combats he has driven off a large
number of enemy machines and has forced down three
balloons, showing a very fine offensive and great fearlessness in attacking the enemy at close range and low altitude
under heavy fire from the ground."*

Bar to the MC
Gazetted 18th October 1917
*"He has destroyed several hostile machines and driven
others out of control. On one occasion he attacked a formation of five enemy machines single-handed and shot one
down out of control; while engaged with an enemy
machine, he was attacked by two others, one of which he
forced down to the ground. He has consistently shown great
courage and initiative."*

Distinguished Service Order
(Later awarded two Bars)
Gazetted 3rd September 1918
Temporary Second Lieutenant (Temporary Captain) E.
Mannock, MC RE and RAF.
*"For conspicuous gallantry and devotion to duty during
recent operation. In seven days, while leading patrols and*

in general engagements, he destroyed seven enemy machines, bringing his total to thirty. His leadership, dash and courage were of the highest order."

Victoria Cross
Gazetted 11th July 1919
"This highly distinguished officer, during the whole of his career in the Royal Air Force, was an outstanding example of fearless courage, remarkable skill, devotion to duty and self-sacrifice, which has never been surpassed."

Aircraft flown by Major Edward 'Mick' Mannock

40 Squadron

Nieuport Scouts 17 and 24 bis
B3607
B1552
B1682
B3554
B3465
B3451
SE5
B665

74 Squadron
SE5a
D276 (also flown at one time by Beauchamp Proctor VC)
D278
C6468
C1112
C8845

85 Squadron
SE5a
E1294

During Training
Vickers FB9 Number A 8601

Other types used by Mannock include the Bristol Scout, DH2, FE8, BAT, AVRO 504. No serials are available for these machines as Mannock's log-book was destroyed.